MW00879290

ADULTING HARD FOR YOUNG MEN

ESSENTIAL LIFE SKILLS TO BECOME INDEPENDENT, WEALTHY, HEALTHIER, HAPPIER, AND GENERALLY A MORE INTERESTING MAN IN YOUR EARLY TWENTIES

JEFFREY C. CHAPMAN

© Copyright 2023 - by Jeffrey C. Chapman – All rights reserved.

The content contained within this book may not be reproduced, duplicated or transmitted without direct written permission from the author or the publisher.

Under no circumstances will any blame or legal responsibility be held against the publisher, or author, for any damages, reparation, or monetary loss due to the information contained within this book, either directly or indirectly.

Legal Notice:

This book is copyright protected. It is only for personal use. You cannot amend, distribute, sell, use, quote or paraphrase any part, or the content within this book, without the consent of the author or publisher.

Disclaimer Notice:

Please note the information contained within this document is for educational and entertainment purposes only. All effort has been executed to present accurate, up-to-date, reliable, complete information. No warranties of any kind are declared or implied. Readers acknowledge that the author is not engaged in the rendering of legal, financial, medical or professional advice. The content within this book has been derived from various sources. Please consult a licensed professional before attempting any techniques outlined in this book.

By reading this document, the reader agrees that under no circumstances is the author responsible for any losses, direct or indirect, that are incurred as a result of the use of the information contained within this document, including, but not limited to, errors, omissions, or inaccuracies.

CONTENTS

To my two wonderful sons, Albert and Aaron,

This book is dedicated to you two amazing young men who have grown up to be successful and independent adults. You no longer need me to tie your shoes, make you breakfast, or remind you to brush your teeth (although I'm still willing to nag you about flossing).

Throughout this book-writing journey, you both provided me with your objective advice and insightful questions, which helped me stay on track and consider different perspectives. Your support means the world to me, and I am grateful for your unwavering encouragement.

I hope this book makes you both laugh, think, and maybe even roll your eyes a little bit (because what's a dad's book without some embarrassing stories?). Remember that no matter how old you get, you will always be my boys, and I will always be here to love and support you, no matter what.

Thank you for being my sons and for making my life brighter and more joyful every day.

INTRODUCTION

It's here! Your search is over, man. This is the definitive guide to saving you from the perils that come with adulting today! I have scoured countless sources and combined them with my own experience in this ongoing war against my inner man-child to bring you the help you need. (There's no judgment here, we all need a little help, sometimes.)

So, dear brother-in-arms, keep this book nearby, and let's learn how to brave this treacherous land of manhood together!

This book will show you the way to find love, fix that leak, tweak that look, and do that trick.

This is the fabled book of adulting hard. *angelic singing ensues*

The guide that will enable any man (no pressure) to survive in this harsh environment and protect those around him.

Who is the Yoda to Your Luke?

First, I'll introduce myself. My name is Jeffrey Chapman. As of this writing, I am 54 years old, I've been married for 30 years, and I have three adult children (twin 26-year-old boys and a 21-year-old girl) and a dog who keeps me on my toes.

In addition to raising our children to become independent, self-sufficient, and happy adults, I also continue to learn and grow every day.

During the pandemic, I learned new talents like being a book publisher as well as how to cook, paint kitchen cabinets and walls, renovate the backyard, and perform other household tasks.

The process of growing up, or "adulting" as they say today, should not only be reserved for kids, but also for anyone constantly learning to accomplish new things as an adult.

The Book for You

This is a guide to adulting for young men, and it includes everything from help with where you live to how you look and act so that you can be the best man you can be. But it doesn't cover *everything* about what it means to be a man. We all find our own way in the world, but by picking up this book, you've already demonstrated that you know there's more to life. That's great, and it's exactly what counts! Every individual should strive for constant self-improvement, and here you will learn some new tricks to help you.

We'll start with the home, then move on in turn to food, your car, your appearance, your finances, your safety, and finally, the way you think and feel. The final four chapters will cover travel and tips on how to interact with people. Finally, we'll try to help you find yourself, your tribe, and your love. Regardless of the kind of person you want to be, this book will help you become a more well-rounded man.

There are a few other sources added too if you need more information, and a list of resources at the end to help. So you can breathe easy, brother. There are ways to help you *adult, hard,* and many are in this book.

CHAPTER 1

YOU'RE ON YOUR OWN... NOW WHAT?

O KAY, THE DAY HAS come. Breathe. You can do this.

Moving out is both exciting and terrifying, but there are a few things you can do and options you have to make this transition more exciting and less frightening.

Where? How? and How Much?

Unless someone in your family is doing it for you, you should probably find a place to live. Don't worry, it's a mission, but it's also a lot easier than you think because there are so many people willing to help. You can get help from a real estate agent, a campus student-living consultant, or a relative. First and foremost, we must determine your budget. Make sure to think about all of your costs, like rent, utilities, groceries, personal costs like toiletries or medicine, a clothing budget, and savings for a rainy day. I created a worksheet to help you figure out your budget. It's part of the bonus material you can download for free at *www.adultinghardbooks.com.*

If you are a student or a young working person, a roommate could be a good option. If you don't want a roommate, a part-time job or a stipend from your parents are good options. As a first-time renter and a younger person, you may not have a credit score yet, so you will need the assistance of a parent in any case. Don't fret though—financial independence will be yours before you know it! In my experience, that was the first thing my sons realized they needed, and by their third year (just like it was in my case a million years ago), they were completely independent.

Meanwhile, as a first-time renter, there are several things you need to know before actually moving in:

Create a renter's profile (it's like the personal details you use when you autofill documents on your phone, but for houses). This will save you a ton of time when you have to apply to multiple places.

Visit the listings in person. You don't want to get catfished by an apartment. Even before you think about applying, use the Google Maps Street View feature to take a virtual tour of the neighborhood and get a sense of what is nearby.

Carefully and thoroughly read your lease agreement. If possible, bring along someone who has been through the process before to help you understand what your rights and obligations are. People who write these things love to use complicated jargon to confuse you and appear intelligent; make sure you research any terms you don't understand. Trust me on this one.

Research your rights. It's great to understand what the laws of your country, state/province, or city can do for you. Don't let anyone take advantage of your youth or inexperience. People tend to not trust young men who are moving out of their parents' house for the first time, and they will try to add additional fees to the agreement to protect themselves. Depending on the case, this might be a form of discrimination. I suggest you cover all your bases before that happens.

Consider getting renters' insurance. People who own homes get homeowners insurance to cover their losses in the event of a fire, burglary, or injury. In every country, cheap options are available, and they are usually a smart investment. Because I didn't know about this type of insurance, I lost my laptop with precious data when someone forgot to lock the gate in a shared house.

Before moving in, please take pictures of every room in your new home. When you eventually move out, a greedy landlord might try to get you to pay for renovations before renting the place again. For example, if the tenant before you left peeling wallpaper and water damage stains on the floor, which you ignored and lived with for a long time, the landlord may try to get you to pay for that. Don't give them a chance. Consider sending the pictures to the landlord before you move in and explain nicely that you don't mind the little faults, but you just want to let them know before you move in. Make sure you keep your receipts. Having proof that you pay your bills every month will help you build your credit score. You will need a stellar credit score to demonstrate that you are a dependable renter and pay your credit cards and utility bills on time. Eventually, that will help you rent or buy a house and a car.

Make sure you get your deposit back. You will need that for your next home. As long as you have the photos, didn't breach the contract, and have repaired any damage or closed up any holes you drilled for the Marvel posters you hung, then you should get your deposit back. Pay close attention to this section of your lease agreement. Typically, it explains what is normal wear and tear and what you must fix before you leave.

Check your lease to see what's included. Some places have utilities like water, gas, Wi-Fi, and electricity included in your rent. But if something is not included, you need to know before you find yourself shivering in the shower because you didn't pay the gas bill. Find out what needs to be fixed and ask if your landlord will pay for it.

If you have one or more roommates, you all need to decide who covers which portion of the utilities and rent. Similarly to the landlord, you should decide these things early so no one is abused.

Make sure your bank, credit card companies, and other vendors, like online retailers or your preferred pizza place, are aware of your current address to ensure that you continue to receive your mail. If you ask the US Postal Service (USPS) early enough, they will also hold your mail. Until you can permanently change your mailing address, they can hold it there for up to 30 days.

Should You Live Alone or Find One or More Roommates?

I've lived alone and I've had roommates, and both are completely different, so let's examine the pros and cons of each:

Pros for living alone:

- You can be completely independent! (Hopefully, Dad and/or Mom will still cover the rent if you're studying).

- You can come and go as you please.

- You can learn how to look after yourself and you can discover who you are as a person, alone.

- House guests don't need any prior announcement or planning before they come over.

Cons for living alone:

- If you aren't very sociable you could get lonely, especially since you were probably used to having people around at home.

- Having one key means you must be responsible and make sure you don't get locked out or lose it. Although you can store a copy in a safe place.

- All the home repairs, chores, watering plants, and feeding the stray cat behind the apartment falls on you.

- Living alone is riskier, whereas having a roommate reduces the chances of being the victim of a crime.

Pros for living with roommates:

- The burdens of the rent and other expenses can be significantly less.

- You have someone to unlock the door and the benefit of safety-in-numbers.

- The housework is split between you and someone else.

- Having more friends implies greater safety and a stronger sense of community.

- Where and How to Find One or More Safe Roommates?

Cons for living with roommates:

- You might fight with your new roommate(s) depending on how well you know each other or which terms you agreed to.

- You must also be fine with their comings and goings.

- Problems can arise when neither of you does your share or just one of you works hard and the other doesn't.

- Uninvited and unannounced house guests could become a real issue. You might also not like having their friends or significant other over or having to fake a smile with them.

If you decide on one or more roommates there are three possible ways to live with others. In the US people can go for an apartment-sharing solution. In the UK a lot of young people (and sometimes older people) are opting for shared houses where they live with many people they didn't know before moving in, much like American fraternities. Still, young, working individuals can also live there (Anonymous, 2022).

In South Africa, they have what are called communes. These houses usually have multiple rooms, and you just rent a room. Considering it is a private home, you usually have someone who fixes things if they break. It is a very cost-effective way to get started.

One option is to live with an old friend or someone you know well. This is a good way to find a roommate because you already know their quirks and habits. However, keep in mind that not every friendship can survive living together. Do a test run first. Perhaps a gaming marathon or a week-long road trip to get a sense of how you'll get along living together. I guarantee there will always be bumps in the road when you spend so much time with someone else, so if you don't want to risk losing your friendship or don't deal well with conflict, then try the next option.

The next option is to find a place and interview a stranger to be your roommate (or find a place that is looking for a roommate like you). However, make sure in both cases you ask the right questions:

- *Do you have any pets?*
  Some people enjoy keeping tarantulas as pets, and if your roommate brings a goliath bird-eater into your room and you suffer from debilitating arachnophobia and a tendency to emit ear-piercing screams, things might get uncomfortable very quickly.

- *What are your favorite and least favorite household tasks?*
  Some people love cooking but hate doing the dishes, or they love laundry but hate ironing. Find some common ground based on what you don't mind doing. Remember, thoughtful compromise goes a long way. You'll have a hard time finding a roommate if you expect them to clean while you just chill. You can ask things like, "Would you mind putting away the dishes while I wash them?" It'll be easier for you two to get into a comfortable rhythm.

- *What kind of music and movies do you like?*
  I know it sounds silly, but when your roommate's Netflix account is filled with horror or rom-com titles and you're obsessed with a compelling drama or action series, things could get sour. Similarly, if you like indie ballads and someone else listens to metal 24/7 at ear-shredding volumes, you can go crazy.

- *Are you a night owl or a morning person?*
  Living with someone who likes to keep odd hours is challenging. If your preferred waking hours are primarily at night and your roommate gets up early,

an unspoken annoyance may begin to develop between you and them. The opposite is also true, as you might want to get up early for a run or the gym while they might enjoy playing games until the wee hours of the morning. Take this issue as it comes, but the best course of action for you both is to make it clear before you move in together.

* ***Do you smoke, drink or take any recreational drugs?***
  Even though it seems like a no-brainer, it's better to have this question out in the open early. If they enjoy cigarettes and you don't, then they will have to go outside every time, since it's your home too. Also, if you like to smoke a blunt every now and then and they are very against it, it may not be the right fit.

* ***How do you feel about relationships? Are you in one?***
  The first time solo living can bring up the issue of partners. No matter whether it's a man or a woman, at home or away, the rules apply. The tricky part is establishing those rules. Since love is blind and messy, figuring out what your roommate wants or already has in the romance department would mean having to deal with it. There's also the sensitive subject of sexual orientation. If you're a member of the LGBTQIA+ extended community and they aren't, or even discriminate against the community, it's best to let them know right away. Having one open and judgment-free conversation can mean a lot.

* ***Would you consider yourself an introvert or an extrovert?***
  It may seem like a small issue, but it all boils down to creating a safe space for all. If you prefer peace and quiet and don't enjoy a very social environment, but your potential roommate is a party animal who has friends coming in and out constantly, things may get unpleasant. Finding out each other's social preferences is good for everyone.

Other questions you should ask may include those regarding food habits, short- and long-term plans, work situations, cleaning habits, financial stability, weekend habits, medium-term plans, and even pet peeves. These questions will help you think about your own situation. Make a list of everything you can think of to make the transition as smooth as possible. I made a handy template to help you get started, and you can find it in the bonus material at *https://adultinghardbooks.com*. Also, don't be afraid to ask your friends for advice on choosing a roommate.

In addition, you could also consult these sources in the references list:

- RentCafe.com Rental blog (Draghici, 2018),

- MyDomaine.com (Knox Finley, 2020)

- TheSpruce.com (Leshnower, 2022)

- Oakhouse.jp (Winston, 2016)

- Dezeen.com (What Is a Share House? n.d.)

CHAPTER 2

KEEP YOUR PLACE FROM CRUMBLING

N ow that you're in your new place, it's time to settle in. So what's next? Make sure it stays in tip-top shape. This section will show you some of the tools and supplies you'll need.

What You'll Need

Here's a handy checklist for tools, bulk items, and cleaning supplies:

Tools:

- A tape measure

- A flat-head screwdriver or a set

- A Phillips ("crosshead") screwdriver or a set

- A hammer

- A rubber hammer

- A wrench or a set

- A spanner set

- Pliers (a side cutter)

- A socket wrench set

- A utility knife ("Swiss Army knife")

- Screws (and their plastic fittings a.k.a wall anchors)

- Nuts

- Bolts

- Nails

- Extra lightbulbs

- Silicone sealant

- Spackle (Filler)

- Sandpaper

- Paint (usually a plain white or the color of your walls)

- A toolbox

- A drill

- A glue gun

- Safety goggles

- Safety gloves

*Note: You don't have to buy all of these in one go. Building a toolbox up to a point where you can do anything is fine. If you get them as you need them that is completely fine.

Cleaning Supplies

- A broom and a dustpan

- A mop

- A bucket

- Cleaning cloths (household use)

- A good floor cleaner (tile-cleaner, wood or laminate cleaner, or carpet cleaner)

- Laundry detergent

- Fabric softener

- Dishwashing soap

- Stain-remover

- A duster

- Dish towels

- A glass cleaner for the shower and mirrors

- Fragrance for the bathroom

- A clothes rack if you don't have an external clothes line or dryer

- Multi-purpose cleaner

- A hand vacuum cleaner (optional)

- Towels for the bathroom

- Bathroom mats

- Rubber gloves (optional)

- Clothes hampers

- A plunger

- A toilet brush

- Toilet cleaner

- Dishwasher tablets and liquid

- Dryer sheets

- Trash cans/ rubbish bins

*Note: Just like with the tools you don't need all of these right off the bat but most of them are needed. If you have sensitive skin or sensitive-skinned pets there are cleaning alternatives like a white vinegar mix that isn't sticky to clean the floors and house.

The Everyday Man's Power Tools 101: From Drilling Holes to Crafting MasterCrapieces

Getting into adulting doesn't mean you'll have to build an entire house, but it does mean taking care of the one you're living in. Understanding basic power tools and how they can help you is essential, even if you're not planning to go full Bob Vila.

1. The Drill: Your Home Improvement Companion

The drill might seem like just a hole maker, but it's essentially the Swiss Army knife of power tools. It's useful in a variety of everyday tasks. Assembling IKEA furniture becomes a breeze, installing a wall-mounted TV is no longer a two-man job, and you can put up curtain rods without breaking a sweat.

When it comes to buying a drill, here's what to look out for:

- **Adjustable speed settings**: This allows you to use the drill for a variety of tasks, from drilling holes in concrete walls to delicately screwing in a tiny screw on a delicate wooden piece.

- **Built-in level**: This can be a game-changer. A level ensures you're not hanging your artwork or mounting shelves at odd, visually displeasing angles.

- **Cordless vs. Corded**: Cordless drills offer greater mobility, but corded drills can provide more power. The choice depends on your needs and the tasks you anticipate.

2. Circular Saw: Your DIY Right Hand

The circular saw might seem scary, but it's a surprisingly versatile tool for an everyday handyman. Want to install a new carpet and need to trim the bottom of your door? A circular saw can handle it. Found some reclaimed wood and decided to build a coffee table? Circular saw again.

Here are some buying tips for your circular saw:

- **Adjustable cutting depth**: This feature allows you to use the saw on a variety of materials and thicknesses.

- **Safety Guard**: Safety should always be a priority. A good safety guard protects you from flying debris and accidental contact with the blade.

- **Power**: Circular saws come in different power levels. If you're just doing light work, a less powerful model might suffice. But if you're planning to cut through thicker or harder materials, consider a more powerful option.

3. The Power Multi-Tool: The Jack of All Trades

Now, let's talk about a tool that truly defines the term "versatile" - the power multi-tool. This isn't just a tool; it's an entire toolbox packed into one handheld device.

Power multi-tools, also known as oscillating multi-tools, are devices that move their attached tool head in a rapid side-to-side motion, like a super-fast scrubbing action. They're designed to take on a multitude of tasks with the simple change of an attachment.

Whether it's cutting, sanding, scraping, or grinding, a power multi-tool has got you covered. Need to cut a small opening in your drywall to install a new outlet? The power multi-tool can do that. Have to remove old, stubborn grout in your bathroom? Yes, the power multi-tool has your back.

What to Look For When Buying a Power Multi-Tool:

- **Power Source**: Power multi-tools come in both corded and cordless versions. Corded versions offer constant power but limited mobility, while cordless versions offer freedom of movement but may require frequent battery changes or recharging.

- **Tool-Free Accessory Change**: Some models require tools to change attachments, which can slow down your work. Look for models that offer tool-free accessory changes for the best convenience.

- **Vibration Control**: Given that these tools work by creating rapid vibrations, they can also transfer those vibrations to your hand and arm, which can lead to fatigue over time. Models with good vibration control or comfort grips can help make the tool more comfortable to use for extended periods.

- **Variable Speed Control**: Different tasks require different speeds, so look for a model that allows you to adjust the speed of the oscillation. For example, you might need a slower speed for delicate tasks and a faster one for aggressive cutting or sanding.

- **Attachments Included**: When buying a power multi-tool, check what attachments are included. Some come with a good assortment to get you started, while others might only include one or two basic ones.

The power multi-tool is a must-have in any adulting toolkit. With it, you can handle numerous household tasks with a single, easy-to-use device. It's a testament to the age-old saying: Work smarter, not harder.

4. Jigsaw: The Craftsman's Secret Weapon

The jigsaw is like the delicate and more artistic sibling in the power tool family. It's the tool you want when you need to cut out detailed shapes or curves in various materials. Want to surprise your significant other with a handcrafted wooden heart? The jigsaw can help. Or maybe you're thinking of making a unique pet door that's shaped like a bone? Jigsaw to the rescue.

When choosing a jigsaw, keep these in mind:

- **Various Speed Settings**: Different materials require different cutting speeds. A jigsaw with adjustable speed lets you work on a wider range of projects.

- **Corded vs. Cordless**: A corded jigsaw usually provides more power, but a cordless one offers mobility. Consider your workspace and the nature of your projects before deciding.

- **Blade changing system**: Some models require tools to change blades, while others have a tool-less system. The latter can save you time and hassle.

5. Impact Driver: The King of Torque

We've all faced that stubborn screw or bolt that just won't budge. It's annoying, time-consuming, and honestly, a little bit embarrassing. That's where the impact driver comes in. This tool is designed to deal with tough screws and bolts that would make a regular screwdriver whimper.

When buying an impact driver, consider these features:

- **Torque**: The higher the torque, the more power to drive screws into tough materials or to loosen over-torqued nuts and bolts.

- **Size and Weight**: Impact drivers are often used in tighter spaces, so a compact and lightweight model can be beneficial.

- **LED Lighting**: This can be helpful for illuminating your work area, especially if you're working in a poorly lit space.

Remember, adulting isn't about becoming a master carpenter overnight. It's about knowing how to handle small repairs and tasks around your home. With these power tools and tips, you'll be well on your way to becoming a proficient DIYer in no time.

Things You Should Buy in Bulk

- Trash bags (get the right size)

- Toilet paper

- Food bags (ziplock style)

- Paper towels

- Batteries

- Cleaning cloths, sponges, steel scrubbers (for the kitchen)

- Tupperware bowls

- Napkins or serviettes

- Containers for pasta, rice, and hot drinks

How to Fix it or Clean it

Some things need to be left to the professionals when it comes to home repairs and even cleaning, but sometimes you can do them yourself and save a lot of money.

You can take care of the following things on your own:

The Clogged Toilet Our Age-old Enemy

When you push down on the lever on your toilet and nothing goes down the drain, take the following steps:

You need to stop flushing.

2. Slowly place the plunger over the hole completely. The idea is to create a tight seal.

3. Slowly push up and down until you hear a big gurgle. You need to be very careful not to splash. A clogged toilet's water isn't something you want to be splashed on you.

4. Lift the plunger and see if the debris goes down on its own. If it doesn't go, try again. Then flush it to get it all cleaned up. If some splashes happen, just wipe them off or get a mop.

5. For the love of everything holy, wash—or at least rinse—the plunger when you're done.

Suction and pressure shift things around until there's enough room for the water and solids to pass through the pipe. Don't flush it again if it doesn't work; that just adds more water to get rid of. Instead, make sure you seal the hole with the plunger and keep pumping.

Dirty Floors or "Gross, What the Hell Did I Just Step On?"

If you like using a mop or broom as a microphone stand while blasting your favorite Queen songs through your speakers, then cleaning floors will be a blast.

I mean, if that's not your cup of tea, get over it. There's no escaping the fact that your floor will need to be cleaned at some point.

The first thing you should do is sweep the area while it's still dry. Make sure you sweep everywhere, even under and behind furniture. The best tip is to dust and wipe off counters first since the floor is the last place everything ends up. Fun factoid: Be careful if you live in South America or in a place where there are superstitions surrounding brooms and feet. Some people think sweeping over their feet will ruin their marriage. You don't want to be responsible for that, do you?

Pour some floor cleaner in really hot water or as directed on the bottle. Don't fill your bucket up. It will prevent accidental spills and be better for your back.

The type of mop you have makes a difference, too. If you have a "spaghetti" mop, you need to swish it in the shape of an infinity sign, trying not to catch it on anything. With a self-wringing squeegee mop, you need to mop forward and backward.

Regularly wring the mop with both hands. It's a great biceps and forearm workout! If you want to get fancy, O-Cedar sells a bucket that uses a foot pedal and centrifugal force to wring the microfiber mop for you. Make sure you don't mop yourself into a corner when you mop. Start at the far end of each room and walk backward so you don't step on the wet floor.

Cleaning the Kitchen Counter and Doing the Dishes

When food goes from plate to mouth, it's awesome. However, if it falls on your kitchen counter on the way to your mouth, it can instantly go from "mmm" to "eww!" unless you clean and sanitize the counter regularly. When you do the dishes, the same effect happens as waterlogged food touches your hands. This, unfortunately, is a fact of life. Cleaning the dishes dirties the water, and you have to put your hands in that water for an effective job.

Gather everything, including pots and bowls, and pile it all next to the sink. Avoid leaving many dishes in the sink daily, as you may become discouraged if you have to take them all out every time before you can start. Next, add hot water and soap to the pots and pans, letting the dishes soak in water to help loosen the tougher dirt.

Rinse first the worst ones. Before you fill the sink, give simpler dishes like plates and bowls a good rinse. Your water will stay cleaner and more hygienic for a longer period if you do this.

After that, fill the sink with hot water and add a few squirts of dishwashing liquid. If you have two sinks, fill the second one with lukewarm water without soap. This is because glass and silverware get water stains if you don't rinse all the soap off. You can dip everything in that sink before putting them carefully on the drying rack.

Depending on whether you have a strong stomach or not, wash all the dishes with or without gloves. Gloves are nothing to be ashamed of; some people have skin conditions, and the soap dries out their hands. Be sure to place the dishes in the drying rack securely so nothing shifts; if you need more space, wipe off a counter and place a dish towel on the counter for mugs, glasses, and pots. Also, put knives in with the blade first for safety. Don't be afraid to refill the soapy basin if the suds are all gone and the water is murky and disgusting.

Finally, wipe off the counters with a sponge and some Lysol or another disinfectant. Keep that sponge separate. It's more hygienic to have two sponges for different purposes, as the same one shouldn't be used for the counter and the dishes. Wipe the oven, microwave, and fridge with a multipurpose cleaner or a vinegar-water mixture. If everything is clean and shiny, you have won the battle. To prevent water stains, wipe the sink too. Also, rinse and hang the dishcloths, while the sponges dry out in a small bowl next to the sink. Place your kitchen sponge under the sink so as not to confuse the two.

Cleaning the Bathroom

When your toilet is dirty, every time you flush it bacteria can be spread through the air. A quality toilet brush is necessary to properly clean the porcelain throne. For all the nooks in the bowl that are more difficult to reach, you would need one that is relatively new and has a broader brush. In the long run, replacing your brush every six months can help keep your bathroom clean.

Other materials required include a bucket, surface disinfectant, disinfectant rags, toilet cleaner with bleach in it, and a sponge or reusable rag. Rubber gloves are an optional accessory, though many people just wash their hands afterward.

The steps to clean your toilet are:

1. Reduce the water level in the bowl, do this by pouring half a gallon of water from your bucket into the back of the bowl. It will trigger a flush and won't fill up again. It is important not to dilute the toilet cleaner, so the goal should be to leave the least amount of water possible in the bowl.

2. Add the toilet cleaner, the bottles of the cleaners come with a swan-like necked squeeze bottle. You can start at the back and squeeze your bottle around the inside of the bowl. You can let the toilet cleaner do its job for 10 minutes while you disinfect the outside.

3. Wipe down the outside, get your cleaner of choice (i.e. rag, sponge, disinfectant rags) and then focus on all the parts of the toilet outside with the surface disinfectant. Make sure to also spend a few moments longer on the handle and seat since you touch them the most. By the time you're done, the bowl should be ready for a scrub.

4. Scrub it well and rinse; keep the brush in the bowl as you securely scrub every part from the lip to the drain. Intently avoid splashing the water around, but be forceful enough to rid the bowl of any stains or debris. When you are finished, flush the toilet to rinse it.

5. Disinfect the brush and its holder, you are nearly finished but a good habit to

get into is to spray disinfectant on the brush itself. Hold it under hot water in the shower, sink, or bathtub, and repeat the process with the holder too. Spray the area where you rinsed it with the disinfectant too for good measure. Place it back next to the toilet when you are done and that would be the end of your duties (Austin, 2021).

Water Problems

If you have a clogged drain; no problem.

First of all, when the drain is clogged, there will undoubtedly be an excessive amount of water in the tub or sink. So, using a bucket, cloth, and mop, remove any extra water. Insects, mold, and bacteria flourish in stagnant water. The water should be removed as soon as possible before any of those lead to unhealthy living conditions.

Second, if the garbage disposal makes a soft humming noise when you turn it on, it means it's stuck. Turn it off immediately and manually move the blades to get it unstuck. There is a special tool that you place under the machine that makes it easier to turn the blades. An Allen wrench also does the trick from the bottom. Be careful, the blades are dirty and sharp. There is the risk of infection if you get cut or even suffer severe injuries. If the clog is anywhere else in the house or you don't have a garbage disposal, then clear obvious blockages with gloves or wash your hands right after.

Third, if there is still a blockage, then boil some water, pour half a cup of table salt into the drain, and then either use the boiling water or get drain cleaner. You can also try a cup of baking soda and a cup of vinegar, then let it bubble for 15 minutes and pour boiling water down. Try other drain-clearing products like Drano, Liquid Plumr, etc. If it still isn't resolved, call a plumber. This may be a job for a professional.

Fourth, if a plumber is out of the question, plunge the drain. Make sure to close all the other drains nearby with a cloth or plug so the pressure is on the clog and water doesn't bubble out in the tub or the sink. After plunging a few times pour more boiling water in.

If you believe the clog is in your sink, place a bucket under the P-trap (the curved section under the sink). Loosen the fittings carefully. After you have unclogged the problem area, reinstall the fittings as you found them. Be careful not to overtighten the slip nuts. You can turn it a few quarter turns with a wrench and your hands. By snaking the drain, you might be able to resolve the issue, but at this point, you might start to think about hiring a plumber. We tried, I know. Not every battle can be won (SeiderTeam, 2018).

Patching Holes on the Wall

 Depending on your lease agreement, you may be charged for patching the holes you leave when you move out. The cost of each hole ranges from $5 to $25.

This is something you should be able to do yourself, so you should learn how to do it.

The process is very simple, don't worry!

Find all the needed materials: spackle, a spackle knife or spatula (the one from the hardware store, not your kitchen), an old credit card or another piece of sturdy plastic, and 150-grit sandpaper. After you have your tools assembled, remove any extra paint flecks or loose sand from the hole.

Then spread some spackle over the hole. Once you have evenly layered it and flattened it with the spatula, wait for it to dry completely. This can take about an hour or longer if you live in a more humid area.

Third, scrape away any excess spackle, but leave a small amount to create a larger bulge off the wall. The edges are your focal points. Use the spatula to even those out until they are level with the wall.

Fourth, sand down the little hill with your 150--grit sandpaper. It is the fine-grit type for the best results. If the hole is still visible you can repeat the process until it is gone.

Fifth, paint over the spot, et voilà! (that's French for: "you done did it, son!") (Stanley, 2020).

A New Coat of Paint

In the very likely case that the color you chose to paint over the spackle is wrong and sticks out like a sore thumb, you might have to repaint the whole wall. If your landlord is okay with it, while you're at it, you might also want to paint the entire thing a different color. Just keep in mind that when you move out, the color will need to be changed back to white, and doing so requires a lot more time and money, especially when going from dark to white. This is how to do it:

Selecting a color is the first step. You can look up color schemes on Google or Pinterest or purchase a color palette at the hardware store, and move around the room experimenting with various options. Measuring the wall or walls will help you determine how much paint you need. For the most part, a quart (36 oz) of paint covers 150 square feet (13.9 meters).

Second, make sure you purchase the right kind of paint for the space. Paint finishes can come in different sheens such as flat, matte, eggshell, satin, semi-gloss, or gloss. Furthermore, indoor and outdoor paint are not the same. To top it off, there is special paint for wood and other surfaces as well. So the options can be overwhelming. Go to the Masterclass website listed in the references to see the different types and their durability, or you can ask at the hardware store (Masterclass, 2021).

Third, put a dust sheet, tarp, drop cloth, or old towels down. Dust and clean the wall with soap and water before you start. Wait for it to dry, then use painter's tape to cover sockets, window edges, baseboards or siding at the bottom, and the edges of the ceiling. You should also get a paintbrush and paint roller (most people get a two-inch brush and a microfiber roller sleeve), primer, soap and water for possible messes, a painting tray (so you don't have to use the can), and if you have high ceilings, a roller extension pole. The last one is so you may reach the top of the wall.

Fourth, depending on the paint type, you may or may not need to use a primer first. After the primer dries, add paint to the painting tray and start painting. Start by "cutting in" the edges with the brush, then use the roller on the remaining flat open spaces. Paint downward from the top. If you roll too fast, you'll end up looking like you have monkey pox!

As much as you can, paint in a space that is naturally lit and well-ventilated. If you use a brush, make sure to remove the shed brush hairs from the wall before the paint dries. Also, don't forget to check how many coats you'll need.

After a 24-hour drying period, remove the painter's tape for the grand unveiling.

Note: Opening and closing a paint can is easily done with a flat-head screwdriver. Be careful not to let it slip and hurt you. If the container is plastic, press down, move forward, hook it under the lid, and then press down. Stand clear while you do this, meaning to just take a step back and lean over so if the screwdriver slips you have time to redirect the arc and not get stabbed (Doherty, 2021).

How to Hang Your Wall Art

Once you ask for the proper permission from your landlord to make holes for paintings, posters, signs, shelves, and photographs, you need to know how to make the holes properly.

The easiest way to hang something is to hammer in a nail. This doesn't work for heavy frames, big clocks, etc. So focus on what you want to hang, its shape, size, and weight, and then what the wall is made of. The drywall is strong enough to hold an 8-inch by 10-inch picture using a single nail, or maybe even a light poster frame. However, for anything heavier, you will need either a wall anchor or a wall stud to hammer the nail into.

Find out if you can drill into brick, tiles, plaster, or paint. Brick is difficult to refinish, but the mortar is easier to fix to get your security deposit back. Tiles may crack if drilled, so avoid them at all costs. Sticky hooks are useful in the kitchen and bathroom.

First, take your pencil and measure with your tape measure where you want it. Remember that you shouldn't make the mark where you plan on looking at the art; you need the mark slightly higher because, of course, your art hangs. Measure from the top down and the sides and the bottom. Be careful not to make too many lines on your newly painted walls. A dot here and there can give you proper guidelines.

Second, get the nails and the hammer. A few quick light taps make a good spot without bending the nail, and the small groove created helps the nail from slipping into your drywall or plaster. If the wall is made of mortar, the same applies. If you have bricks, the landlord may have a problem with holes in their wall. If you have the go-ahead, try it the same way, but first, research how you would go about fixing the holes when you move out to weigh the pros and cons.

Third, you can hammer in the nail properly, but be as gentle as you can with the nail so as not to bend it during the process. Hammer it in at an angle until it is stable, but remember to leave room for the frame wire or string. If you are unsure, a quick test when you pull down slightly on the nail can show its stability.

If you have a white plastic art hook, you can hammer it in and hang art. Make sure all three nails are in the plastic so they don't damage the art. Put a towel or bag down to catch dust, or sweep it up.

Use a drill, plastic-cased screws, or wall anchors for heavier art. Drill straight through the screw's plastic casing with a drill bit of the same size. Drill in small increments, testing the depth with the screw as you go. Once the hole is deep enough that the casing enters the point before expanding, tighten the screw with a screwdriver. Be sure to leave room for the wire to hang on, and then hang your art. Clear the dust made by the drill from the floor and appreciate your art as well as your great handiwork.

If you're interested in a full course on home repair and improvement you can check out this great course from Udemy. Just click on the link or scan the QR code.

Comprehensive Home
Repair and Improvement

What Does This Button Do?

Since the beginning of time, men have been great at taking things apart. Nonetheless, we appear to be surprisingly perplexed by the simple operation of the most common electric appliances in the home. This is a crash course on how to use your household appliances properly:

How to Use a Dishwasher

You'll need:

- a dishwasher (I know... genius!)

- dishwasher tablets (optional)

- dishwasher liquid (optional)

- dishwasher gels (optional)

- dishwasher powder (optional)

For the type of tablets, liquid, gel, or powder needed, you can search the web for the best kind for your specific brand and type of machine. Tablets work the best, according to most sites. Gels should be a last resort. In the machine, liquid can work with baking powder, but if used alone, it may wash away before any cleaning is completed. Powder also washes out quickly, but it is the less expensive option that still works.

Never use regular dishwashing detergent in a dishwasher. You'll have a mountain of foam on your kitchen floor to deal with! And it's not fun at all, no matter what my dog thinks.

Depending on the type of dishwasher you have, there is a place for any of the types of soap. The tablets gradually break down in the washing process, so they work well, but all types of soap create suds and get the job done.

After scraping the solid food from the dishes, open the machine and stack them. There is no need to rinse the plates; dishwasher soap works better when it can cling to food particles. Plates, pots, and pans are placed at the bottom. Glasses go at the top, and silverware goes at the bottom or the very top in their own trays. Graters and wooden spoons can be stored wherever there's room. When stacking the dishes and silverware, be sure not to cover the rotating sprayers, either at the top or bottom, sometimes both.

Make sure everything faces the center of the machine.

Second, before closing, there is a little panel on the inside that clips open for the two soaps. The square bit is for tablets, powders, or gels, and the liquid goes in the little circle after you open a plug. The amount of liquid varies, so you can add three or four drops and baking powder to the rest of the space.

Third, you have to figure out the array of settings. Turn it on by pushing the power button, then see which of the washes you want. The easiest option is to look for a quick-wash setting. If you are stumped, you can ask the landlord for the user manual or search the internet for the specific dishwasher's reviews, tips, and booklet.

How to Use a Washing Machine:

You'll need:

- Your laundry without anything in the pockets

- Laundry detergent

- Fabric softener

- You guessed it: A washing machine

Separate your white and lighter clothes from anything with color. Then you can open the hatch at the top or front and add your laundry. Be sure not to overload the machine as it won't wash properly when overloaded.

Once your laundry is in, add a lid's worth of the fabric softener bottle to the little pull-out tray. It goes in the middle or on the right side of the tray. Then, add a scoop of laundry detergent. Most bags include a measuring scoop. If you have a big load, you may need two scoops, but be careful; if you add too much soap, it gets starchy and white crystals can stay on the clothes, which are difficult to get off after the clothes dry. The detergent goes in the left tray or on the clothes themselves. Some people add a little white vinegar to the rightmost tray if you have one. It kills bacteria, and many stains are gone with vinegar including blood and armpit stains. *Note: Some older machines, like the ones at laundromats, don't have a space for your detergent or softener so you can just pour it directly into the machine.

Third, close the tray and turn on the machine. Look for a quick-wash option or a 30-minute wash.

Fourth, you can use the rinse and spin cycle to remove any remaining detergent. You can skip this step if you're trying to save water and you're confident that you didn't use too much detergent. Your clothes are now clean.

Fifth, remove the clothes and hang them up or place them in the dryer.

Please keep in mind that some fabrics shrink in the dryer. The tags show what different materials can handle. Furthermore, a cold wash shrinks clothes, so use at least lukewarm water. Some clothes also have dye that comes off in the wash during the first few washes after buying them. So first, wash new clothes in a tub or basin with detergent. This is why we separate our whites and colors before washing them. I recommend you do that every time to make sure your white T-shirts and underwear don't come out tie-dyed.

How to Use a Dryer:

You'll need:

- your freshly washed clothes

- a dryer

- dryer sheets

First, put the clothes in the dryer. They should only be damp and not drip on the floor as you transport them from one to the other. Wet clothes actually damage dryers.

Second, toss the dryer sheets into the machine. For bigger loads, you can use two sheets.

Third, start the dryer and set it to regular or heavy for your everyday clothes and a cooler setting for your delicates, e.g., scarves, hats, or cashmere sweaters.

*Once again, read the clothing tags before putting them in the dryer. Most sweaters and dress shirts shrink.

How to Use an Oven:

You'll need:

- an oven

- the food you want to bake, roast, or broil

- a pot, tin pan, or glass bowl

- oven mitts or a kitchen towel

- baking paper, aluminum foil, and a silicone liner (optional)

First, decide what setting you'll require. The oven must indeed be preheated, but what do the other symbols mean?

A square with a line at the bottom
Turns on the lower element, which gently heats food from the bottom, making it ideal for stews, casseroles, and crisping pizza bases and pastry cases.

A square with a line at the top and at the bottom
Turns on both elements, allowing heat to be applied from both the top and bottom. This feature is used to bake scones, bread, pastries, and roast meat.

Three dots with a line under them

The bottom element and the fan are both turned on, which means that direct heat from the element is circulating through the oven. It's great for keeping things moist on top but crispy on the bottom. This method can be used to make pastries on pies, crispy pizza bases, and quiches.

A circle around three dots

The fan is on but it has its own circular heat element at the back of the oven (not all ovens have this element). This circulates the heat from the back and a range of food can be cooked this way. It works best for meat that you want tender on the inside and nicely roasted on the outside.

Two squiggly lines at the top

The full grill is turned on. Because the grill function is the hottest, we use it to cook bacon, sausages, other meats, and toast. We also use this function at the end of some dishes to add that extra crispiness. Examples include lasagna, shepherd's pie, and various meat dishes.

One squiggly line

Only half of the grills are on. This function is best used on the uppermost level, closest to the grill, and is used to broil meats and cheeses.

One squiggly line with three dots below it

Half of the grill and the fan are turned on. The grill's high temperature is evenly distributed throughout the oven. This method can be used to cook fish and tougher meats.

One squiggly line with a line at the bottom

The bottom element and half of the grill are turned on. This indicates that an even heat is coming from the bottom and a high heat is coming from above. The method can be used to make crisp base and brown top pizzas, tarts, and pies.

A snowflake with a water droplet under it

This is the defrost mode. If you forgot to take the food out of the freezer earlier, it will defrost quickly.

A lightbulb

Turn on the oven light. Some ovens lack this feature and only have a light when the oven is turned on. This function can be used both while cooking and later when cleaning the oven.

Three lines curved at each end

It is the setting to warm your plates. It is to ensure that your plates are slightly heated in order for the food to stay warm for a longer period of time.

Nine circles: 3 small, 3 medium, and 3 big

This is the pyrolytic cleaning function. This is similar to incineration in science fiction films. A 500-degree temperature burn-off cleans your oven. After that, simply wipe away the ash.

A small bell

This is the alarm. It helps you set that ever-important check-in time.

A clock

This is the minute-minder mechanism (say that three times fast). This function turns off the oven after a set time.

A key

This is the child safety lock. It is usually found on the stovetop, but sometimes ovens have this function too. When you turn it on, the oven and stove will not respond to the dials or buttons until you disable them. It's good for pets, too.

Some ovens don't have any of these symbols and only have two dials. One dial serves as a timer, while the other displays temperatures with the grill function at the bottom. When using these ovens, 350 degrees Fahrenheit or 180 degrees Celsius is ideal for most food types. The recipes can give you a good idea of the temperatures required.

• • • ● ● • ● ● • •

Deco-rating: 5 Stars

Home design varies according to individual preferences, but there are a few elements that can transform any house into a cozier home.

Consider the following suggestions to complement your style:

- **Possibly a plant on a table** near the entryway helps you stay organized and looks great. This allows you to unwind while keeping the outside where it belongs.

- **Consider getting more pillows and throws.** Throw pillows and small blankets known as throws are used to make a space appear cozier and more inviting. These pillows are also textured and affordable, so they go with everything.

- **Include plants that complement your aesthetic.** Try succulents or cacti for a neat minimalist look. Add some tall ferns or bougainvillea if you have a more eccentric taste. They're all easy to care for and look great in a variety of colors.

- **Paint with colors that best reflect your style.** Minimalism uses pure, cool, and light colors. A room can look bigger and cleaner if it is painted a light gray or a muted blue. If you prefer warmer, pastel colors, a light orange or a faded red can make your home look welcoming. Do some research on your color preferences and incorporate them. It's your home, so make it your own!

- **Think about window treatments.** Window dressings do a lot to make a house feel like home while also adding privacy. Blinds, also known as shades, are ideal for achieving a clean look. Heavy-patterned drapes complement warmer tones and are ideal for adding a splash of personality.

- **Play with light.** Try adding a standing lamp, fairy lights, LED lights, neon, or any other light options you can think of. Consider how you feel when you see a house that has been beautifully decorated for the holidays. It has the same effect as when a house appears well-lit on the inside. It is a simple upgrade, but it has a significant impact.

- **Look into layered furniture**, that is, furniture that serves multiple functions and can provide additional storage space. If your coffee table has lots of storage for linens and books or if your sofa can pull out to accommodate guests, you have an extra makeshift bedroom. A good rule of thumb is to get as much storage space as possible while keeping your areas separate. Your desk should be for work; then you can focus when you sit there and foster good habits.

- **Get an end table near the front door.** Keeping your mail, keys, and comfort level in your home goes through the roof!

- **Put up some artwork.** If you want larger art on your walls, frame some posters or create some original art. Otherwise, think outside the box. You can add a hanging shelf for books and keepsakes. Not all art pieces have to be conventional, thick-framed, ornate oil paintings.

If you're interested in a full course on how to accessorize your place like a pro, you can check out this great course from Udemy. Just click on the link or scan the QR code.

Design is in the Details:
How to Accessorize Like a
Pro

CHAPTER 3

DON'T STARVE TO DEATH!

Y OU FINALLY HAVE YOUR apartment for you and your friends to eat whatever you want. Your kitchen is a treasure trove, waiting to be discovered and explored. But what meals should you prepare? What do you need to make them? Where is the kitchen again? Don't fear; this chapter includes some recipes and every kitchen utensil you might need.

I made all of these myself, and even the ones that look the most complicated can be made in about an hour. Don't forget that I didn't know how to cook before the pandemic. Even water burned when I heated it.

Your Kitchen Utensils

Here's a guide to some kitchenware you might need for your culinary endeavors:

- Silverware

- Plates and bowls (You can choose how many but a set of four is a good start. Four big plates, four small plates, and four bowls.)

- Glasses and other glassware (See chapter nine for drinks you can make and their different glasses.)

- Measuring spoons

- Measuring cups

- A chef's knife. Don't skimp on this one. This is going to be one of your best kitchen friends, so get the best one you can afford.

- A spatula

- A pasta spoon

- A ladle

- A whisk

- A slotted spoon

- Kitchen sheers

- Tongs

- A thermometer

- A non-stick pan or skillet

- A saucepan

- A sheet pan

- An immersion blender

- A colander or strainer

- A box grater

- Prep bowls

- A cutting board

- A can opener

- A wok (optional)

- A vegetable peeler

- An Instant Pot (consider this one seriously. You can make so many things quickly and easily)

- Oven mitts

- Kitchen towels

- A paper towel holder

- A toaster oven or a toaster/air fryer combo

- A well-stocked spice rack (start small and work your way up. In the kitchen, spices are your best friend.)

- Pot stands

- A knife set

- A bottle opener

- Baking pans (A bread pan or a muffin pan depending on if you enjoy baking)

- A basting brush

- Big mixing bowls

- Mugs and cups

- A bamboo steamer (If you like to or would like to cook Asian cuisine)

- A silverware tray for the drawers

- A kettle

- Wooden spoons

Here are some foods you should consider always having on hand:

- Rice

- Pasta (Fusilli, spaghetti, macaroni, etc.)

- Tomato sauce

- Bread

- Buns (the kind you like, e.g. paninis, cheese, etc.)

- Muffin mix

- Cake mix

- Oats or other breakfast cereals

- Meat (You can't go wrong with chicken breasts, beef steaks, ground beef, bacon, etc.)

- Cold cuts and/or sausages

- Vegetables you like (Mixed frozen vegetables, potatoes, carrots, onions, mixed frozen country vegetables, etc.)

- Garlic (Keep garlic on hand at all times). This will be used in a variety of recipes and will last a long time in a drawer).

- Onions (Onions, like garlic, are used in a variety of recipes, both raw and sautéed, so keep a few on hand)

- Produce you like (apples, bananas, tomatoes, avocados, etc.)

- Baking powder

- Baking soda

- Phyllo (filo) pastry dough roll

- Confectionary sugar (optional)

- Butter (Salted for sandwiches, unsalted for baking)

- Milk (Depending on your dietary needs, almond milk is a good substitute if you are baking and adding milk to food)

- Cheese (American, cheddar, feta, brie, and gouda are all good)

- Sugar

- Salt

- Pepper

- Olive oil

- Instant noodles

- Soup powder

- Parmesan cheese

- Bread crumbs

- Flour

- Self-raising flour

- Some snacks (Chips, candy, etc.)

- Canned foods (tuna, baked beans, etc.)

- Chicken and vegetable broth

Condiments:

- Soy sauce

- White vinegar

- Worcestershire sauce

- Ketchup

- Mustard

- Sweet chili sauce

- Mayonnaise

- Herbs and spices (Cumin, cayenne pepper, oregano, paprika, mixed herbs, rosemary, thyme, ground cloves, curry spice, turmeric, salt/pepper/garlic mix, etc.)

- Cream (this spoils quickly, so only buy it if you intend to use it frequently and soon)

- Jellies and jams

- Peanut butter

- Marmite or Bovril (Australia, the UK, and South Africa)

This is by no means an exhaustive list. You can get whatever else you want. Don't be afraid to substitute ingredients you don't care for, and don't be afraid to leave things out if you don't want to use them while cooking.

The Taste Test

Some simple recipes can make you appear to be a professional chef. Here are some dishes that will impress both your taste buds and your guests.

If you can master a few dishes that you enjoy, you'll be able to entertain your friends and family at the drop of a hat.

Quick Meals:

Air Fryer Salmon

If you have an air fryer and want to prepare a quick and super healthy meal, you can't go wrong with this salmon. It takes about 20 minutes and comes out tasting amazing!

Here are the ingredients you'll need:

- 2 (6-oz.) salmon fillets

- Kosher salt

- Freshly ground black pepper

- 2 tsp. extra-virgin olive oil

- 2 tbsp. whole grain mustard

- 1 tbsp. packed brown sugar

- 1 clove garlic, minced

- 1/2 tsp. thyme leaves

Instructions:

1. Sprinkle salt and pepper over the salmon.

2. Mix oil, mustard, sugar, garlic, and thyme in a small bowl.

3. Spread over salmon.

4. Place the salmon in the air fryer basket.

5. Cook for 10 minutes at 400° Fahrenheit (205° Celsius). Enjoy!

Stir-fry With Yellow Rice

Here are the ingredients you'll need:

- 1 cup/person stir-fry frozen vegetables (or if you can't find the pre-packaged mix then carrots, zucchini, bell peppers, mushrooms, and anything else you like, chopped in strips)

- 1 tbsp. soy sauce

- 1 tsp. of salt

- 1 tbsp. olive oil

- ½ tsp. pepper

- Beef, chicken strips, or shrimp (if you're feeling fancy)

- ½ tsp. cayenne pepper

- 1 onion

- 1 cup/person rice

- 1 tsp. turmeric (add another for every cup of rice)

- 1 tsp. mixed herbs spice

You will also need:

- 1 wok or pan

- 1 small pot (Change to a bigger pot for more than two people)

Instructions:

1. Cut the onion and measure out your vegetables. One cup of frozen vegetables is a healthy portion size but adding more gives you a second helping or some leftovers. If you have to cut your beef or chicken because it isn't prepackaged as strips then cut the chosen meat too. Shrimp is already the right size.

2. Add the pot to the stove filled to about three-quarters with water.

3. Then add the salt and mixed herbs.

4. Pour in the rice (one cup per person but more is always better). Lastly, add a tablespoon of turmeric to the rice.

5. Switch on the stove element, on about 3 or 4. This is on medium heat. If you have a gas stove then allow the flame to start and keep it to a lower heat.

6. Add some oil to the wok or pan and heat it on medium heat. See step 2 for the different heating options above.

7. Add the meat, vegetables, a tablespoon of soy sauce, and half a teaspoon of all the spices except the turmeric together in the wok or pan.

8. Stir everything as it cooks making sure to keep the heat to a point where the oil doesn't spray out.

9. When the meat and vegetables are crisped on the sides take the stir-fry off the heat. See that the rice has enough water to keep it from burning as you cook. (That means pour more water in as soon as you hear it sizzle and little holes appear between the grains of rice where the steam comes out.)

10. Allow almost all the water to evaporate from the rice when they get soft. (We keep a little water in so we don't burn the rice and for more moisture.) Serve the stir-fry on the rice.

Chicken Fajitas

Fajitas are a tasty and easy weeknight meal. In less than 30 minutes, you can whip up this delicious Mexican recipe. If you prefer, you can substitute shrimp for chicken.

Here are the ingredients you'll need:

- 3 boneless skinless chicken breasts
- 1 onion (thinly sliced)
- 3 bell peppers (thinly sliced)
- 2 tbsp. olive oil
- ½ lime
- ½ tbsp. chili powder
- ½ tbsp. ground cumin
- 1 tsp. garlic powder
- ½ tsp. paprika
- ½ tsp. oregano
- ½ tsp. salt
- ¼ tsp. pepper

- tortillas

- sour cream

- pico de gallo (chopped tomatoes, onions, serrano or jalapeño peppers, cilantro, and lime juice)

- avocado

Instructions:

1. Mix the fajita seasoning ingredients in a small bowl.

2. Cut the chicken into 1-inch strips. Apply fajita seasoning generously to both sides of the chicken or shrimp.

3. Heat oil in a large skillet. Cook chicken breasts for 7-8 minutes on each side.

4. Slice your bell peppers and onions while the chicken cooks.

5. Let the chicken or shrimp rest for a few minutes after it has finished cooking.

6. Stir frequently while sautéing the bell peppers and onion over medium heat. For extra flavor, sprinkle the remaining mix.

7. Mix the chicken or shrimp back into the skillet with lime juice.

8. Serve immediately with tortillas and extra toppings such as sour cream, pico de gallo, and guacamole.

Gourmet Meals:

Chicken Pie

<u>Here are the ingredients you'll need:</u>

- One roll of phyllo (filo) pastry

- Flour

- 3 or 4 chicken breasts

- 1 cup of mushrooms

- 1 cup of mixed vegetables

- 2 big potatoes

- Soup mix

- 1 cup of milk

- 1 egg

- Salt

- Pepper

- Cayenne pepper

- Parmesan cheese

- Mixed herbs

- Butter

- Cooking spray

- Any other spices you might like

- A pot

- A glass baking bowl

- A pastry brush

Instructions:

1. Chop the potatoes and chicken breasts into bite-sized pieces. Slice the mushrooms. If the phyllo pastry was frozen, defrost it.

2. Fill the pot halfway with water and add the spices.

3. Heat the pot until it's boiling and add the vegetables, mushrooms, and chicken. Add some butter too for extra flavor.

4. Spread some flour on the counter and use some of it to coat your hands as you unroll the phyllo pastry while the filling is still in the pot.

5. To slightly flatten the dough evenly, either use a dough roller or your hands. Don't make it too thin or it will tear. Next, spray the glass baking bowl outside or in a well-ventilated room.

6. After measuring the dough beneath the bowl, cut a piece of it off. Cut it slightly larger than the bowl so that it is larger than the top. The dough piece should then be positioned at the bottom of the sprayed bowl and draped over the sides. Make sure there is no air under the dough so that it is flat and can accommodate all of the filling.

7. Put the bowl in the oven on very low heat to bake the base of the pie slightly. This should take around 10 to 15 minutes.

8. Finish the filling by mixing ¾ of the milk with the soup powder in a mug before pouring it into the pot. The soup should thicken the mixture but if it is still too runny for a pie filling, mix a little water with flour in the mug and pour that in little by little until it thickens properly.

9. When the filling is done turn off the stove and move the pot to the side so it can cool while you measure the dough again for the top of the pie. This is the exact

size of the bowl base.

10. Break the egg in a mug and use the other ¼ of the milk, beat it together.

11. Then pour the filling into the base of the pie. Put the other dough for the top over that and brush the egg mixture over the top to make sure it browns well.

12. Place the pie in the oven at 350 degrees Fahrenheit or 180 degrees Celsius. When the pie bakes to a golden brown color it is finished. Clean up while the pie cools and then enjoy it.

Instant Pot Barbacoa

This Instant Pot barbacoa (Mexican shredded beef) tastes like it was cooked low and slow all day, but it can be made in less than 2 hours. This dish will make you famous among your friends. I guarantee it!

Here are the ingredients you'll need:

- 3 pounds beef chuck (cut into 2-inch pieces)

- 3 tbsp. vegetable oil (or as needed)

- ½ cup chicken stock (or beef stock)

- ⅓ cup apple cider vinegar

- ¼ cup lime juice

- 2 chipotle peppers (in adobo sauce, minced)

- 2 tbsp. adobo sauce (from the peppers)

- 1 tbsp. ground cumin

- 2 tsp. dried oregano

- 1 ½ tsp. kosher salt

- ¾ tsp. ground black pepper

- 2 bay leaves

Instructions:

1. On the Instant Pot, select the sauté button and add about half of the oil. Add about half of the beef when the oil is hot. Brown all the sides. Place the beef on a plate. Continue with the remaining oil and beef.

2. In a bowl, combine the stock, vinegar, lime juice, peppers, adobo sauce, cumin, oregano, salt, and pepper. Add the liquids and seasonings to the pot and stir, scraping up any browned bits in the bottom of the pot.

3. Add the beef back to the Instant Pot along with the bay leaves.

4. Place the lid on the Instant Pot and lock it in place. Turn the valve to the sealing position and select pressure cook or manual (high pressure). Set the timer for 45 minutes.

5. Let the pressure come down naturally for about 10 minutes. To release the remaining pressure, turn the valve to venting.

6. Shred the beef with two forks in a pan or bowl. Add the liquids to the beef.

7. Serve the beef in soft or crisp corn tortillas with fresh salsa, lime wedges, and chopped cilantro.

10 Easy-to-Make Appetizers and Their Recipes

1. Classic Bruschetta

Ingredients:

- 1 baguette

- 2 cups diced tomatoes

- 1/4 cup chopped fresh basil

- 2 cloves of garlic, minced

- 2 tablespoons olive oil

- Salt and pepper to taste

Instructions:

1. Combine the tomatoes, basil, garlic, and olive oil in a bowl. Season with salt and pepper. Let it sit for about 15 minutes.

2. Slice the baguette into 1/2-inch pieces and toast until golden.

3. Top each slice with the tomato mixture.

2. Garlic Parmesan Wings

Ingredients:

- 2 lbs chicken wings

- 4 cloves garlic, minced

- 1/2 cup grated Parmesan cheese

- 1/4 cup melted butter

- Salt and pepper to taste

Instructions:

1. Preheat your oven to 400°F (200°C).

2. Toss the wings in the melted butter, garlic, salt, and pepper.

3. Spread them out on a baking sheet and bake for 40 minutes or until crispy.

4. Sprinkle Parmesan cheese over the wings and bake for another 5 minutes.

3. Bacon-Wrapped Dates

Ingredients:

- 24 pitted dates

- 12 slices of bacon, cut in half

- 24 toothpicks

Instructions:

1. Preheat your oven to 375°F (190°C).

2. Wrap each date with a half slice of bacon and secure with a toothpick.

3. Place the dates on a baking sheet and bake for 20 minutes, or until the bacon is crispy.

4. Caprese Skewers

Ingredients:

- 24 cherry tomatoes

- 24 small mozzarella balls

- 24 fresh basil leaves

- 24 skewers or toothpicks

- Balsamic glaze for drizzling

Instructions:

1. Skewer a cherry tomato, a basil leaf, and a mozzarella ball onto each skewer.

2. Arrange the skewers on a platter and drizzle with balsamic glaze.

5. Guacamole

Ingredients:

- 2 ripe avocados

- 1/2 small onion, finely chopped

- 1 Roma tomato, diced

- 1 jalapeño, seeds removed and finely chopped

- 2 tablespoons chopped fresh cilantro

- Juice of 1 lime

- Salt to taste

Instructions:

1. Mash the avocados in a bowl.

2. Mix in the onion, tomato, jalapeño, cilantro, lime juice, and salt.

3. Serve with tortilla chips.

6. Spinach and Artichoke Dip

Ingredients:

- 1 cup chopped spinach

- 1 cup chopped artichoke hearts

- 1/2 cup sour cream

- 1/2 cup cream cheese

- 1/2 cup grated Parmesan cheese

- 1/2 cup shredded mozzarella cheese

- 1 clove garlic, minced

- Salt and pepper to taste

Instructions:

1. Preheat your oven to 350°F (175°C).

2. Mix all the ingredients in a bowl and transfer to a baking dish.

3. Bake for 20 minutes or until golden and bubbly.

7. Mini Meatballs

Ingredients:

- 1 lb ground beef

- 1/4 cup bread crumbs

- 1/4 cup grated Parmesan cheese

- 1/4 cup chopped fresh parsley

- 1 egg

- 2 cloves garlic, minced

- Salt and pepper to taste

- Your favorite marinara sauce for dipping

Instructions:

1. Preheat your oven to 400°F (200°C).

2. Mix all the ingredients (except the marinara sauce) in a bowl and shape into 1-inch meatballs.

3. Place the meatballs on a baking sheet and bake for 20 minutes or until cooked through.

4. Serve with warm marinara sauce.

8. Stuffed Mini Bell Peppers

Ingredients:

- 12 mini bell peppers, halved and seeds removed

- 8 oz cream cheese, softened

- 1 cup shredded cheddar cheese

- 1/2 teaspoon garlic powder

- Salt and pepper to taste

Instructions:

1. Preheat your oven to 350°F (175°C).

2. Mix the cream cheese, cheddar cheese, garlic powder, salt, and pepper in a bowl.

3. Stuff each pepper half with the cheese mixture.

4. Place the peppers on a baking sheet and bake for 20 minutes or until the cheese is melted and bubbly.

9. Shrimp Cocktail

Ingredients:

- 1 lb large shrimp, peeled and deveined

- 1 cup ketchup

- 1/4 cup horseradish

- 1 tablespoon Worcestershire sauce

- 1 tablespoon hot sauce

- Juice of 1 lemon

- Salt and pepper to taste

Instructions:

1. Boil the shrimp in salted water until they turn pink, about 2-3 minutes. Drain and chill.

2. Mix the ketchup, horseradish, Worcestershire sauce, hot sauce, lemon juice, salt, and pepper to make the cocktail sauce.

3. Serve the shrimp with the cocktail sauce.

10. Hummus and Veggies

Ingredients:

- 1 can chickpeas,rinsed and drained

- 2 cloves garlic

- 2 tablespoons tahini

- Juice of 1 lemon

- 1/4 cup olive oil

- Salt to taste

- Assorted raw veggies for dipping

Instructions:

1. In a food processor, combine chickpeas, garlic, tahini, lemon juice, olive oil, and salt. Process until smooth.

2. If the hummus is too thick, add a tablespoon of water at a time until it reaches your desired consistency.

3. Serve the hummus with raw veggies such as carrot sticks, cucumber slices, and bell pepper strips.

These appetizers are not only easy to make, but also delicious and perfect for any occasion. Happy cooking!

Desserts:

Coffee Fudge Cake

Here are the ingredients you'll need:

(for the cake)

- 4 tbsp. margarine

- 5 tbsp. caster sugar

- 1 egg

- ⅖ cup of self-raising flour

- ½ tsp. instant coffee

(for the icing)

- ⅖ cup of icing sugar

- 2 tbsp. of butter

- 1 tbsp. water

- 2 tbsp. sugar

- ½ tsp. instant coffee

- Measuring cup

- Measuring spoons

- 6″ (15 cm) in diameter cake pan

- Mixing bowl

- Wooden spoon

- Small bowl

- Small saucepan

- Paper towel

Instructions:

1. Grease the pan with margarine using a paper towel. Sprinkle some flour in the pan after that.

2. Combine 4 tablespoons of margarine and 5 tablespoons of caster or granulated sugar in a mixing bowl. Using a wooden spoon, blend.

3. Crack an egg into a small bowl and whisk it with a fork.

4. As you add the butter-sugar mixture, pour it in gradually.

5. Using a wooden spoon, combine it.

6. Mix in ½ tsp. of instant coffee.

7. Sieve the ⅖ of self-raising flour over and fold it in. Pour it into the cake pan and bake it for 20 to 25 minutes at 350 degrees Fahrenheit or 180 degrees Celsius on the oven's top rack.

8. Do the dishes while you wait.

9. Allow the cake to cool. In a small bowl, sift 2 1/2 cups of confectionary sugar. Turn on the stove.

10. In a saucepan over low heat, combine 2 tbsp. of butter, 1 tbsp. water, and 2 tbsp. sugar.

11. Once the sugar has melted, continue stirring.

12. Add the boiling mixture to the icing sugar as it bubbles.

13. Add 12 tsp. of instant coffee. Stir it until it becomes spongy after allowing it to cool.

14. Then apply it to the cake.

Pancakes

Here are the ingredients you'll need:

- ⅖ cup of flour
- Salt
- 1 egg
- 3 tbsp. milk
- 2 tbsp. water

- 1 tsp. olive oil

- 1 tsp. cooking oil

- ⅕ cup of sugar

- ½ tsp. of cinnamon

- 1 lemon

- A measuring cup

- Measuring spoons

- A mixing bowl

- A smaller mixing bowl

- A wooden spoon

- An egg beater

- A sieve

Instructions:

1. Sieve the flour into the mixing bowl, and add a pinch of salt. Make a hole in the middle of the flour and add the egg, 1 tbsp. milk, and olive oil. Stir it with a wooden spoon.

2. While you stir, add the rest of the milk and 2 tbsp. of water then use the egg beater.

3. Turn on the stove and add 1 tablespoon of cooking oil to the pan.

4. Pour the oil into the small bowl. Save enough oil to cook the pancakes in.

5. Pour the mixture into a measuring cup with a lip you can use to pour from and stir it once more for good measure.

6. Pour it in until the edges of the pan are covered.

7. Bake it fast until the bottom slightly turns brown. You'll know when the edges start lifting and move it when you shake the pan.

8. Then flip it with a spatula. If you want to try and flip it without then make sure there is something that can catch it underneath if it fails.

9. Mix the sugar and cinnamon, sprinkle it over the pancake, and cut the lemon. Honey is also delicious with it and add a slice of lemon on the top as decoration.

10. Bake the rest of the pancakes with the remaining batter. It should be enough for three. Double or even triple the recipe ingredients to make more.

Healthy Snacks:

Peanut Butter Protein Balls

Here are the ingredients you'll need:

- ⅔ cup old fashioned oats

- ¼ cup unsweetened shredded coconut

- 2 tbsp. mini chocolate chips

- 1 tbsp. chia seeds

- 1 tbsp. flax seeds

- ¼ tsp. ground cinnamon

- pinch of kosher salt

- ⅓ cup natural peanut butter

- 2 tbsp. honey

- ¼ tsp. pure vanilla extract

- 2 tbsp. milk

Instructions:

1. Line a large baking sheet with parchment paper. In a large bowl, add the oats, coconut, chocolate chips, chia, flax, cinnamon, and salt.

2. Stir in the peanut butter, honey, vanilla, and 1 tablespoon of milk.

3. The mixture should be slightly crumbly. If it's too dry, stir in up to 1 more tablespoon of milk little by little.

4. With wet hands, roll the mixture into small balls and place them onto a baking sheet.

5. Put them in the fridge until they are chilled, 30 minutes.

(Miyashiro, 2018)

Air Fryer Sweet Potato Fries

Here are the ingredients you'll need:

Fries:

- 2 medium sweet potatoes, peeled and cut into ¼ " sticks

- 1 tbsp. extra-virgin olive oil

- ½ tsp. chili powder

- ½ tsp. garlic powder

- Kosher salt

- Freshly ground black pepper

Dipping sauce:

- 2 tbsp. BBQ sauce

- 2 tbsp. mayonnaise

- 1 tsp. hot sauce (such as Texas Pete)

Instructions:

Fries:

1. In a large bowl, toss sweet potatoes, oil, chili powder, and garlic powder until evenly coated; season with salt and pepper, then toss them again.

2. Working with a few at a time, in an air-fryer basket, arrange the sweet potatoes in a single layer.

3. Cook at 375° Fahrenheit (190° Celsius) for 6 minutes, flip the fries, then cook until browned and crispy, 5 to 8 minutes more.

Dipping sauce:

1. In a medium bowl, whisk BBQ sauce, mayonnaise, and hot sauce together.

2. Put the sweet potato fries on a platter.

3. Serve with the delicious dipping sauce.

(Abraham, 2019)

How to Be the Host With the Most

If you host a small gathering at your new place, it will give you the chance to show off your culinary prowess. Here are a few pointers to consider before you set out:

When You Go to the Grocery Store

Is that squishing sound good? How to pick your produce.

- You can't go wrong with **vegetables** as long as the exterior is flawless and the texture is firm.

- You can tell if a **fruit** is ripe by its color and aroma; if it doesn't smell at all, it's not ready yet; if it smells sour, it's past its prime; and if it smells fresh, you're in the right ballpark.

- You should wait until the **bananas** are fully ripe before eating them if they are still a little green. Its ripeness can be gauged by the number of brown spots it has.

- If an **avocado** is deep green and soft then it is ripe and should be eaten as soon as possible.

- If **apples** are soft and wrinkled, steer clear as this means they are overripe and if your watermelon is white in places it's overripe, as well.

- The lightest part of a **watermelon** should be yellow.

- Check for bruises and mold near the stems of any **berries** you intend to purchase. If that's the case, then they're no longer in pristine condition.

- To determine whether a **fruit** or **vegetable** is ready to eat, look at its weight in relation to its size; if it's disproportionately large, it's likely ripe and juicy; otherwise, it's probably still immature.

- Consider the season as well. There is no better time to buy than when a fruit or vegetable is in season.

Is this organic?

When should you spring for organic, and when should you save your money?

When it comes to organic products, they can be quite pricey. However, if you buy from a farmer's market or directly from an organic farmer, the price will be lower.

When those options aren't available or feasible, sometimes more is less. For example, buying a whole organic chicken makes sure that everyone in the house gets their favorite cut and that there are enough leftovers for sandwiches. You can also use the broth. This way, you can skip the store-bought stock or soup powder, which saves you money.

Organic foods are also significantly less expensive when they are in season. If you find a lot of organic berries at a good price, buy some and bake with them. You can preserve them by adding them to tarts or frozen desserts, or by making jams or jellies. This will reduce the need for additional sugar, jam, jellies, and ice cream.

Avoiding ready-to-eat organic meals will also help you save a lot of money. It makes sense; if it takes the producer more time and money to get it to you, it will cost more; however, if it is the raw product, you will have to use more of your energy to prepare the meals, but it will be less expensive and you will gain some skills.

Because organic products are more expensive, you must decide where to cut and where to keep them. Make wise financial decisions without allowing them to rule your life.

A good rule of thumb is: For anything you eat with the peel on (e.g., apples, pears, strawberries, berries, peaches, bell peppers, celery, lettuce, kale, tomatoes, spinach, etc.), buy organic as it probably has more pesticide residue when it is not organic. For anything you peel or cook (e.g., potatoes, pineapple, bananas, kiwis, avocados, melons, watermelons, corn, onions, eggplant, etc.), organic is less necessary.

Twenty apples add up. When to buy in bulk?

The average American consumes 53 pounds of bread per year. (SouthFloridaReporter.com, 2017). Bread spoils quickly, but it can be frozen, so if you have some bread in your freezer after purchasing it in bulk, you are making wise choices. Do this with as many items as you can if you have the space.

If you know you eat a lot of popcorn, buy a lot of it as a snack. It's a healthier alternative to chips and cookies. See where else this mindset can be applied and put it to use right away.

Many people buy 24 eggs rather than just 6 because they last longer, and in a fridge, you can stack bread and other items on top of the carton while still having a proper breakfast every other morning.

Is that a six or an eight?

Carefully check expiration dates.

The terms **"Best before"** and "Use by" are important to understand. A product's "Best before" date indicates how long it will maintain its peak freshness; however, it is generally safe to consume the product a little longer after this date.

The **"Use by"** date, typically found on meat packaging, indicates the latest possible consumption of the product without health risks. Stores typically move newer items to the back and older items to the front to sell them first. A good tip is to always look at the back of the shelves at the store to see if there are any items with a longer expiration date.

Be cautious when traveling abroad; some countries write the date differently (e.g., Day/Month instead of Month/Day), and others put the date of manufacture instead. (In China, the production date is printed on the packaging in addition to the suggested shelf life, so you'll have to figure out when the product will go bad on your own).

If you're unsure about the date format, it's best to ask a local.

(Best Before, Use by, and Sell by Dates Explained, 2021)

Finding the best value for your money.

We discussed what to buy in bulk and whether or not to get organic produce on a tighter budget, but there are other ways to make your money go further.

Most stores have house brands, also known as "private label," which means the brand is owned by the store; for example, a Costco fruit juice labeled Kirkland. Common grocery stores often have their own house brands of food that are slightly less expensive than name brands. In the United States, Trader Joe's and Costco come to mind; in the United Kingdom and Australia, Tesco is a prime example. These house brands sell for a lot cheaper than the other products and can save you quite a bit of money.

Get a loyalty card and keep an eye out for sales. Having a rewards card can help you save both on bundles and on individual items.

Some helpful tips for the kitchen:

- Choose recipes with overlapping ingredients.

- Some ingredients overlap in the recipes above but don't be afraid to find your tastes and see which flavors go well together.

- You can use beef or chicken in both a starter and a main.

- Costs can be reduced by using the same butter called for in the cake recipe, the pasta sauce, or the puffs used in the appetizer.

How to prepare your staple foods

Depending on your staple food, it is possible to make a mistake in the preparation stage. Not all staples are created equal, and there are subtle differences that, if overlooked, can leave a bad taste in your mouth.

Rice

1. Rice is an easy staple to prepare.

2. You can start by washing your rice.

3. Just rinse it in a bowl and pour out the water through a sieve.

4. Then measure a cup of rice per person and two cups of water for every cup of rice.

5. Add the rice and water to a pot.

6. Stir it, add some salt and herbs and then put a lid on before turning the stove plate on high.

7. Let the water boil and the rice cook.

8. Use a fork to gently mix the rice when it's done so it doesn't get too soggy or mushy.

Pasta

Cooking pasta is a little more difficult because you have to add the water to the pot with a little bit of olive oil, salt, and herbs, then bring it to a boil before you add the pasta.

Remember to keep the flames at a manageable height when working on a gas stove because some pasta, such as spaghetti, can burn if it hangs over the side or sticks out of the water and touches the hot rim of the pot. If the pasta is soft and sticks to your hand after cooling, strain it.

Throwing it against a wall is a messy testing method. Simply take a piece and taste it after it has cooled. When you bite into it, the center of the pasta should be slightly whiter than the rest, indicating that it is al dente.

The term *al dente* refers to slightly harder pasta; many people believe that this is the best state for the pasta to be in because it is not too soft but also cooked, allowing for a more stimulating texture.

Mashed Potatoes

Mashed potatoes are a classic dish. The potatoes can either be peeled before boiling or after they have split open in the water.

To give the water more flavor, add some salt. If you intend to peel them after boiling, let them cool first; otherwise, your kitchen will become the scene of a painful game of hot potato.

After peeling the potatoes, season them with salt, pepper, garlic, and rosemary, as well as a tablespoon of butter and a small amount of milk. You can then mash them up more or less until they are lumpy or extra fluffy, depending on your preferred texture.

If you took my advice and got an Instant Pot, you could make mashed potatoes in about 20 minutes. Just put the potatoes in the Instant Pot, add 3/4 cup of water to the pot, and cook for 10 minutes. Then mash the potatoes right in the pot and add the milk, butter, garlic, etc.

To Freeze or not to Freeze, That is the Question

Freezing is an excellent way to preserve food for a long time. If you do most of your cooking for one, you will probably make way more than you need. Unless you intend to eat only a small number of the meals you prepared during your weekly meal prep session each day, it's a good idea to eat some and freeze the rest.

I highly suggest investing in a **vacuum sealer** if you have the cash on hand (roughly $60 to $120). The only thing worse than thawing out two weeks' worth of leftovers is discovering that they taste like the inside of the freezer.

However, you can't freeze everything you buy or make. Listed below are some suggestions for what to store in the freezer and what to devour as soon as possible.

Don't Freeze These:

Leafy greens. Their capillaries will burst, transforming them into a soggy translucent version of themselves. The majority of water-rich produce does not freeze well.

Sauces and gravies. If they are bonded with starch, they will become watery when used again.

Pudding. For the same reasons as sauces and gravies.

Neither **dairy products** other than cheese nor soups with a cream base freeze well. They may split apart or curdle.

Non-fatty fish shouldn't be frozen after cooking because it can become waterlogged.

Cooked staples, when defrosted, have the same problem as leafy greens.

Cooked egg whites, without the yolk, will have a rubbery texture.

Mayonnaise, sauces, and dips containing mayonnaise will separate like oil and water.

Freeze These:

Cheese freezes well as long as it is tightly wrapped or vacuum-sealed. It will last up to two months.

Meat. Most types freeze well. However, do not thaw and refreeze it more than once.

Eggs can be frozen if they are first cracked and beaten. Never put an entire egg in its shell in the freezer.

Other types of **soup**, as long as they are water-based, can be frozen without problems.

The best **vegetables** to use if you are unsure of their water content are premixed frozen vegetables, although mushrooms, broccoli, and other vegetables with low water content also keep very well.

However, cooked, mashed, or sweet **potato** must be thoroughly cooked first.

Products with eggs baked in, like quiches, egg tarts, cakes, etc.—are all fine to freeze.

Bananas freeze really well and can make tasty frozen treats.

(Cammarata & Eating well, 2022)

If you are unsure about other things like butter (yes, you can freeze butter) then you can research the specific product. Some things only freeze well if they are sealed up tight and others only when they are cut first or in a meal.

Want to take your cooking to the next level? Check out this great cooking course from Udemy right here. Just click on the link or scan the QR code.

Essential Cooking Skills

CHAPTER 4

GET A SWEET RIDE AND KEEP IT SWEET

WITH ALL THE OPTIONS out there, you need to be well-informed before you get a vehicle, especially since this is another big purchase that you will probably make a few times in your lifetime.

Buying vs. Leasing — New vs. Used:

Pros for buying a new car

- Brand new car. less maintenance. Includes mileage-based service plan

- You get to make all the choices.

- Except for your payments, there is no deadline to worry about.

Cons for buying a new car

- It is pricey. A brand-new car automatically depreciates the moment you drive it off the lot.

- You must pay and learn about maintenance. It may also incur additional costs such as sales tax, smog checks, and any additional features you choose to pay for.

- You are more constrained because, once you have the car, you must live with your choices.

Pros for leasing

- In the short term, it is less expensive than buying.

- It is much faster than purchasing your own car as buying your own car is a very extensive, time-consuming process.

- You can get a better car than you could have gotten if you had bought a new car.

Cons for leasing

- The car must be returned at the end of the lease term.

- All of the decisions and rules are not yours to make.

- You must be extra cautious, and cleanliness is essential, as some places will penalize you if your car is dirty.

Pros for buying a used car

- Used cars are cheaper. You could get the remaining service plan visits as well.

- More options You should buy an older model if you like it.

- Because fixing it up will not void the warranty, your customization options are greater.

Cons for buying a used car

- When purchasing a used car, it is impossible to know for sure if it is in excellent condition.

- If you get a used car, get a diagnostic sheet from a mechanic or take a mechanic along to do an inspection. This is another extra cost.

- Parts can be difficult to come by. Some manufacturers stop producing parts for older models.

Make it Run Without Running Out

Tips when buying a car (new or used)

Choose a dependable vehicle, research your brands, and begin with a clear idea of what you want, but be willing to compromise.
Some of the most reliable (and affordable) brands are Toyota, Mazda, Honda, Subaru, Kia, Hyundai, Nissan and Volkswagen. There are many good cars on the market, and if you keep your options open and your ear to the ground, you will undoubtedly find something you like.

Do the research and determine the budget.
Going to different dealerships, researching prices online, and discussing prices with others can give you a good idea of how much it will cost. Both new and used cars have costs that can be reduced or eliminated. As an adult, you may want your dream car, but it is usually not the most affordable or best option at this point in your life. A car will get you to your destination faster and will open doors to your future. A white knight can ride in on a donkey if it means he has a palace and can provide for himself, his friends, and other loved ones in the long run. Try not to become fixated on the most expensive option. Weigh the pros and cons, look at different options, and find something that works for you and your budget.

Before you go to the dealership, arrange for financing.

"Before" is the key word here. Even if the financing options at a dealership are good, you might be able to get a better rate at a different bank or credit union. Remember that the extras will be more expensive. So, if you buy a slightly less expensive car, you can get things like electric windows or a roof rack if you really want them.

Shop around at various dealerships and plan to spend the whole day buying a car.

Trust me. When you walk into the first dealership, you should already have another location in mind. This ensures that you get the best deal possible. Anyone who enjoys shopping will tell you that there are other options. You never know if a salesman is just being a smooth-talking businessman or if they truly have your best interests at heart because most people have quotas to meet and bills to pay. They want to upsell and can spot a novice buyer a mile away. Having options allows you to protect yourself.

Negotiate the best possible price.

And be prepared to walk away. By simply leaving, you can learn the dealership's absolute lowest acceptable offer. You'll know they're not willing to take a financial risk on you if they let you go. Cars are sold by the most charismatic people, and you should strive to be just as charismatic. It's best to begin with a low number and work your way up to your ideal price. One that is ideally lower than your limit. This doesn't always work out perfectly, but when it does, you have a new car and extra cash for gas and other essentials.

Test drive the car.

Seeing how the car feels and handles while driving can make the choice for you. It is best to test drive any vehicle first to see if your leg space is enough, your seat is comfortable, etc. This will ultimately lead to a more informed and justified choice.

Don't buy unnecessary extras.

As mentioned earlier, the salesperson needs to make ends meet too, and will do everything in their power to get more out of the deal. That means tinted windows, tire, and wheel protection, maybe a different, more-expensive color, and so forth. You can listen but don't let them strongarm you into unnecessary extras. Focus on the fact that you don't have a car before and any car is better than none. You can always add extras later when you make some more money.

Have any used cars inspected.

The final section of this chapter discusses what you can and cannot fix yourself on your car. Things that you can't fix yourself are complicated or dangerous. Thus, it is a great idea to take a qualified technician with you before you buy a used car. They are aware of the pitfalls and can help you avoid them. A diagnostics sheet is what a mechanic uses to check all kinds of things about a used car. This assessment tells you everything you need to know to make a good choice.

Evaluate the value of your trade-in.
Similar to the previous point, you should check the value of your car before trading it in for another. Find someone who knows the ins and outs of the business to help you, and make sure your car is in good shape.

If you are buying a new car, look into the manufacturer's rebates.
Throughout the year, many car companies offer rebates and other incentives. Do a quick search on Google and have the results ready for the seller. Then they can't be coy, and you might get a better deal.

Instead of looking at the monthly payment, look at the total price.
If you focus on the bigger number, the finance manager can't try to trick you into thinking that the smaller prices are the only ones that matter. They usually try to get the customer to focus on the monthly payments because they know it's easier to close the deal on their terms if the payments are affordable. Instead, throw them a curveball, and you may end up with lower monthly payments or a smaller total amount.

Pay attention to and finish one part of the deal at a time.
The four-square worksheet that the finance manager uses bombards you with all of the numbers at once. They tell you all at once the value of your trade-in, the total cost of the car, the down payment, and the monthly payment. Refuse to be overwhelmed by the numbers and insist on going through them one by one, starting with the total price and then, if you have them, the trade-in amounts before you look at the other two. Remember, everything is negotiable.

Ask the finance manager to list every fee.
There are so many fees, and sometimes they are just there to make more money for the financial manager. Negotiate every fee. For example, the documentation fee can be worked down from $100 to $75. Don't just take any fees at face value. Question

everything.

Negotiate the rate on your loan.

They try to make more money off the loan as well. After the thorough research you've probably done, they shouldn't be able to fool you, though. If they offer a higher percentage than the bank, then mention it and ask for a lower percentage on their end.

Don't buy unnecessary extras.

Some of the extras they try to sell you are things you can do yourself for less than $30, like scotch-guarding the inside or etching your VIN on the windows. Don't fall for it. Instead, ask for a moment to talk to a trusted friend or family member, and then look up the add-ons to see if you really need them. You don't need to spend hundreds of dollars more when you're already paying so much for your car. Remember that the finance manager is the best salesperson at the dealership. They have perfected their sales pitch over the years and will try to convince you that everything they are selling is a must-have.

Take the time to carefully read through the contract.

Ask for 30 minutes to read the contract and don't feel like you have to hurry. They shouldn't be in charge of how fast the sale goes. You're the customer who's spending a lot of money. Get out of their office, circle the things you don't understand, and if they try to avoid explaining the things you circled by saying things like "Don't worry about it," tell them, "If I don't need to worry about it, why is it in the contract at all?" If they don't seem to have time for your questions or the sale, remember that this is another way to get you to not look at the fine print. They can't be in such a hurry to turn down all of your money.

Figure out the contract amounts yourself.

There may be a difference in the amounts, and sometimes this is done on purpose. Do your own math and ask about any numbers that don't make sense.

Don't give in to pressure to buy right away.

This is a huge financial choice, so if you need more time, make sure you get it. If they put a time limit on the sale, don't fall for it. Either they won't sell the car you want, or they'll have something similar enough that it won't matter. Take all the time you need or go to a dealership that will respect you *(Hamby & Mueller, 2022)*.

Don't Leave the Lot Without It!

Car insurance is a necessary evil. It's better to have it and not need it than to need it and not have it. Plus, minor detail: It's illegal to drive without it.

Because you're still young and haven't been driving for a long time, expect to pay a lot more for car insurance than someone with a clean driving record.

So, what do you need?

First, let's understand what each term means:

Deductible: This is what you pay out of pocket before the insurance kicks in to cover a loss. When you buy car insurance you need to decide how much you are willing and able to pay with your own money in case of an accident. The lower the deductible, the higher the premium.

Premium: This is what you pay every month for insurance coverage.

Your policy covers three basic things: liability, comprehensive, and collision.

Liability coverage: This covers the costs of any medical expenses or repair costs you cause to someone else in an accident. Almost every state in the US, except New Hampshire and Alaska requires you to have this. If you live outside the US, check your local laws. But, to be honest, even if it wasn't the law, it would be very irresponsible of anyone not to carry this type of coverage. How much Liability Coverage should you get? Get at least $500,000 USD.

Comprehensive coverage: This protects you in case your car is stolen or damaged in a fire, flood, or another natural disaster. If you own your car, this is not required, although I recommend you have it, especially if your car is fairly new. If you are leasing your car, the finance company will require you to buy this coverage to protect their asset.

Collision coverage: This covers the costs to repair your own car. It is not required by law but you must have it if you are leasing the vehicle. If you are driving a very old car and you have the cash to replace it in case of a bad accident, you may want to skip this coverage. Otherwise, I recommend you get it.

These are the main three types of coverage. However, you will see other terms such as uninsured motorist, GAP, rental reimbursement, pay-per-mile, umbrella, roadside assistance, etc.

The more important ones are:

1. **Uninsured (or Underinsured Motorist)**: This coverage protects you in case you get hit by someone who is not properly insured. Yes, even though it's the law, many people take a chance and drive without insurance! Some states require you to have this type of coverage.

2. **Guaranteed Auto Protection (GAP) Insurance**: If you get a loan to buy a new car and something happens to it, the insurance company will cut you a check for the actual market value of that car. However, you might still owe more than the car is worth. And you will still need to pay off that loan. This type of insurance covers that gap. The smart financial decision would be to buy a used car you can afford. But if you decided to splurge and get a loan, get the GAP insurance and try to pay off the loan as soon as possible.

3. **Rental reimbursement**: As the name implies, this coverage lets you rent a car while yours is being fixed after an accident. If you really depend on your car and you don't want to pay for a rental out of your pocket, you might consider getting this.

4. **Roadside assistance**: This will help you when you get a flat tire (and you don't have a spare), run out of gas, have a dead battery, etc. This type of service, provided by companies like the American Automobile Association (AAA), Nationwide, Travelers, and others can come in handy when you need it the most.

5. **Umbrella insurance**: Also known as personal liability insurance, this is an extra layer of protection that covers things the other coverages don't, like legal fees, false arrests, etc. If you have a high net worth (over $500,000) this type of insurance will protect your assets in case of an accident. You probably don't need

it... yet (Ramsey Insurance, 2022).

Getting Your Hands Dirty

You may be able to fix certain issues with your car on your own, which will save you money and give you some serious street cred. Look over these frequently occurring auto problems and decide which ones are within your comfort zone.

Changing a Tire

1. **Spare me.**
   Take out the spare (it is usually in your trunk under a panel), and don't forget the jack and wheel spanners. It's important to remember that spare tires aren't always included with brand-new automobiles, but they are becoming increasingly common. For example, Ford gives customers the option of purchasing a spare tire separately from the vehicle. Some manufacturers, including Toyota, insist on a spare tire being kept in the vehicle at all times.

2. **Loosen the nuts.**
   Before you start jacking, give each wheel nut a quick once turn to loosen them slightly because once in the air the wheel will turn and you will find it difficult to loosen the nuts.

3. **Jack it up.**

The jack consists of the handle and the flat, expanding part that does the actual lifting. See your owner's manual for the correct location to place the jack under the vehicle. You then begin turning the handle until the car rises. Please be cautious and place it close to the edge of the car without risking it sliding off. Make sure the car and jack are on a flat surface.

4. **Now you can go nuts.**

In other words, loosen the nuts on both ends until they can move freely. The phrase "lefty loosey, righty tighty" was the best piece of advice I've ever received. NEVER risk getting under the car on your own, as there's always the chance it could topple on top of you at any time, ruining your whole morning. You can remove the wheel after you loosen the nuts. Be wary of any nearby street drains; you wouldn't want your nuts to disappear into the sewer system.

5. **Tired yet?**

The bolts and nuts can be tightened across each other after the spare tire has been mounted. Following the clockwise sequence of numbers from one to six: You would go first to four, then two, six, three, and finally five. Please ensure they are properly tightened.

6. **Drop it.**

You can slowly jack the car back down and then tighten the nuts again. Put the flat tire back in the trunk, and don't forget your tools! Make sure to get the old tire fixed as soon as possible.

This is critical: If you have a spare tire, you should not drive for long distances or at high speeds with it. Spare tires are not intended to replace regular tires, but rather to assist you in safely reaching a tire shop.

Oil Check and Changes

An oil change is not something you should attempt unless you know what you're doing. This process is complex and outside the scope of this book.

However, knowing when it's time to change your oil means getting an oil check. You can handle that by yourself. To get a precise reading, it is best to check the oil when the vehicle is cold. Every 10,000 to 15,000 miles (16,000 to 24,000 km) or every six months, you should change the oil.

Included in the bonus materials is a car log that will help you keep track of your car's maintenance. Just visit *https://adultinghardbooks.com* to get it.

The owner's manual will be helpful, as some modern vehicles lack a conventional oil dipstick in favor of an electronic oil monitoring system. It's best to do this with the car on a flat surface, with the engine cold so you don't risk getting burned, and with the oil in its thicker state.

Once the engine is turned off, you can pop the hood and access the oil dipstick. You should clean the stick of any excess oil before using it. Then, insert it back into the tube and push it in all the way. Depending on your vehicle, the oil gauge may look different. For any system of measurement, the minimum and maximum values are represented by two lines. If the oil level is in the middle, or near the top, everything should be fine. Keep an eye on the shade; if it's not brown or black, coolant may be leaking into the oil, and metal fragments may indicate internal damage. Tow the vehicle to the nearest repair shop if you notice any signs of coolant leakage. Go see a mechanic regardless if you see either of these signs. If everything looks good, you can close the hood and put the dipstick back in.

If it's getting low, then you need to top off the oil. The best oil to use is specified in the manual. Oil is sold at gas stations, auto-parts stores, and even some supermarkets. To add oil, you need to take off the engine's oil cap, use a funnel, and pour the oil in slowly so as not to overfill the engine, which can cause serious damage. Occasionally stop and check the dipstick as you move around. When it's at the right level, replace the cap securely and close the hood. If you need to add more than a quart of oil, however, it's time to see a mechanic.

Battery

If something clicks over and over when you turn the key or push the button, or if the car won't turn on at all, your battery is probably dead or bad. Don't bother checking it out yourself; instead, contact a mechanic or roadside assistance professional. Avoid attempting repairs on it yourself, as exposure to battery acid can cause permanent eye damage or skin burns if it gets on you. Never attempt to repair your own battery.

Wipers

You can easily replace them on your own if they fail to wipe the water away and prevent you from seeing in the rain.

1. Raise the wiper arms up; do this by releasing the clip at the back of the wiper. If you push the wiper in the direction of the glass, it will slide out.

2. Replace your worn wiper blades with new ones of the same length and mounting clips by visiting any auto parts store. You can also find them online for your specific make, model, and year of the vehicle.

3. Replace them in the exact reverse order that you removed them. Attach them to the wiper arm and lower it; however, take care not to let the arm drop without the wipers in place, as doing so can cause damage to the windshield.

Air Filters

They need to be cleaned or replaced every 12,000 to 15,000 miles (20,000 to 25,000 km) in the city, and every 3,000 to 6,000 miles (5,000 to 10,000 km) in rural areas. It's best to take it to a mechanic because replacing them is tricky. It's not dangerous, per se, but it is challenging and you could break them.

Brake Pads

Do not attempt repairs on your own; a mistake could have fatal consequences. Brake noise or a spongy sensation when applying the brakes is a signal that you need to visit a mechanic.

Jump Starting a Car

Jump-starting a dead car can be tricky, but once you know the process, it's very straightforward:

1. Place the two cars so that their front bumpers are touching or side by side.

2. Put on the parking brake for extra security.

3. Open both hoods and locate the batteries. You may need to remove the protective plastic coverings to gain access.

4. Locate the battery's positive and negative terminals. Be sure that there is no corrosion present.

5. Connect the red clamp to the positive post on the dead battery.

6. Connect the other red clamp to the positive post on the working battery.

7. Connect the black clamp to the negative post on the working battery.

8. Connect the last black clamp to an unpainted metal surface of your car.

9. Turn on the vehicle with the charged battery, let it run for two to five minutes, and then try to turn over the other vehicle with the jumper cables still attached. This shared voltage will allow both cars to start, and the alternators will keep each car running.

10. You should disconnect the jumper cables but leave the second car running once it starts. Drive to a mechanic to make sure the alternator, battery, and other parts are fine.

Car batteries can and will fail over time. Or they will be drained if you leave your indoor light on all night by accident. Always keep a set of jumper cables in your trunk. They cost around $20 USD, take up little space, and will come in handy when you need them. Another excellent option is to purchase a self-contained jumpstart battery that does not require the presence of another vehicle. They are about $60 on Amazon.

Water

Your car's temperature has risen too high; what should you do now? Check your water. But make sure it has cooled down completely. This is because water and steam at high pressurized temperatures can cause severe burn injuries during decompression.

1. Open the water cap as directed by your user manual, but it is also written on the cap.

2. Fill it up with water and add some antifreeze. Antifreeze or coolant keeps your car's water from freezing while also cooling it in hotter climates. It has elemental resistance, which prevents it from exceeding certain temperatures and reduces corrosion in the water system. The amount to add is usually indicated on the coolant bottle.

3. Replace the cap securely.

Fuel and Fuel Type

This one isn't really a fix; just check your owner's manual to see what fuel type is recommended for your specific vehicle. Because diesel and gasoline have different chemical bases, using one in an engine that is tuned for the other could seriously harm your vehicle.

• • • ● ● ● • ● ● • ● • •

If you want to learn more about simple car maintenance you can do yourself, check out this course by clicking on the link or scanning the QR code below.

Car Maintenance Anyone
Can Do

CHAPTER 5

YOU'RE AN ADULT. FEEL THE PART, LOOK THE PART!

WHEN YOU FIRST ENTER the adult world, you may have trouble "feeling the part" because you are saddled with so many responsibilities and so many people are counting on you to make the best decisions for yourself and your future. Discovering one's own identity is half the fun. Your goals, ambitions, and dreams are taking shape, and if you put in the effort, you can make them all come true.

Setting Your Goals

You can brainstorm a plan to reach your goals. It's normal to lack clarity on your long-term objectives, but most people find clarity once they commit to a plan. You can express your hopes and dreams for the future in a variety of ways; some people create aspiration boards, while others keep diaries or create works of art. Whatever path you choose, working little by little to achieve your goals makes them attainable.

Personal goals are more manageable than aspirations because they are more concrete and often come with a deadline. People often say things like, "I want to be married by the time I'm 28" or "I want to have kids before I'm 30." These goals are fine, but smaller, more easily attained goals give you a sense of progress and maturation. Making your bed first thing in the morning can give you a small sense of control over your day. That can apply to your career, love life, and intrapersonal relationships. There are a hundred little fires you have to put out before you can call yourself a firefighter, but once you put out that one fire, the rest of the goals become much more manageable. That is not to say that you shouldn't aim high. You can get there more quickly if you have a clear endgame in mind and set attainable intermediate goals.

Objectives are steps you take to realize your desired goals. If you hope to open a restaurant someday, a reasonable goal would be to locate an appropriate spot, and a reasonable objective would be to consult with a real estate agent before the end of the month.

A mission is a set of objectives and goals that lead to the realization of a dream.

Here are some pointers for setting goals:

- **Identify your passions.**
  Discover your true motivations and what really excites you. They will not hold if they do not inspire you.

- **Realistic goals.**
  The most successful goals are those that are both attainable and within your control. The pressure to succeed increases when the outcome is in your hands, but your dedication will see you through. When the outcome depends on the actions of another person, your plans may not come to fruition.

- **Write them down.**

  To remind yourself that they are still in your life when things get rough, keep some physical reminder of them close by.

I've included a goal-setting worksheet in the free bonus materials at *https://adultinghardbooks.com* that will help you think of ideas and get clearer.

• • • ● • ● ● • •

Manscaping and Man-buns – Self-care

Your you'nique style

Some men spend years perfecting a particular hairstyle, while others give in to whatever their hair feels like doing on any given day.

Since you are no longer dependent on anyone else, you are free to explore your personal style. Don't be surprised if, in a few decades, you find yourself desiring a bowl cut just because Thor did it in some alternate universe. That's perfectly fine, by the way. In the end, it's your body.

If you're curious about the effects of experimenting with color, go ahead and give it a shot. If you want to experiment with a new hairstyle or color before making a permanent commitment, you can do so with the help of one of the tens of mobile apps.

A shorter cut that requires less maintenance daily is great if you're not a fan of spending time on your hair. Get a nice leave-in conditioner or a conditioner to use every other day if your hair dries out quickly. It's recommended that you wash and condition your hair more frequently the shorter it is. Additional natural oils are required for longer hair.

When it comes to facial hair, it is best to wait until you can grow a full beard before growing it out and concentrating on beard style. Still, you have the right to do whatever you want with your body. If you want to grow a mustache because that's all you can grow, that's fine. Fortunately, it can be quickly and easily shaved off if you decide you don't like it.

The best thing you can do for your skin is to use a product that doesn't contain alcohol after you've shaved. There are beard oils that can make it smooth, but some of them can cause skin irritation, so you'll have to experiment to find the right one.

If your beard grows in unevenly, you could try micro needling with a derma roller. Micro needling may facilitate better beard hair growth by increasing nutrient-rich blood flow to the area, in addition to activating collagen and keratin production. The same goes for hair and skin health: good circulation is essential for both.

There are complete nose-to-tail trimming sets available with adjustable clippers, so you can shape and stubble your beard and hair as you see fit.

A hairy situation

Some men have too much hair. Tweezing your unibrow is a simple way to make yourself look much more put-together than you are.

When it comes to manscaping, the conversation gets more complicated. Many men are self-conscious about their hair, but some embrace it. Having an excessive amount of hair can be both unsightly and irritating. If your hair is getting in the way of your activities or your partner's, it is acceptable to shave occasionally. The only rule is to do it for your own sake and not anyone else's.

It should also be mentioned. You can shave your backside to save toilet paper and have a cleaner undercarriage. A trim or shave at the front for comfort and an overall better appearance is also a good idea. You don't have to, and remember that hair everywhere is natural for some men. There is no reason to feel any way about it. It's just that having a pair of scissors on hand for when your armpits or other body hair becomes excessively long is a wise practice as you get older.

Creams, gels, mousses, and soap

I'm going to let you in on a little secret: Men have skin too. Yeah, I know... crazy, right?

A good skin and hair care regimen are essential to look your best. A basic skincare regimen begins with twice-daily face washing. Wash your face first thing in the morning to remove any leftover dirt and impurities from the night before, as well as sweat and bacteria. Also, wash before bed to start the nighttime routine. The second step in the skincare routine is to exfoliate twice a week. This removes dead skin cells, brightens the skin, and treats acne. Exfoliate after washing your face at night and before applying moisturizer. Which is the third and final step in your skincare routine. However, you will require two types of moisturizers. The first is for use during the day, keeping your skin hydrated and providing SPF protection, and the second is for use at night. The moisturizer keeps your skin looking and feeling young. (Nast, 2022)

The differences in hair products are determined by your hair type, hair length, and personal preferences. Longer hair requires treatments such as a hair mask or the use of proper cleaning and conditioning products. To style it, we usually use less gel and more mousse or even hairspray. Short hair does not require much maintenance, but avoid using gel, wax, or mousse daily. Your hair needs to rest from time to time. Gel is used to create a wet appearance and hardens and crusts over time. Wax provides a stronger hold and can appear wet or dry depending on when it is applied (if you apply it while your hair is wet that is the look you get, whereas if it is only a little damp you get a drier look). Mousse is used to achieve a dry matte look. Most people prefer wax or gel, but these can damage your hair faster, so don't overdo it.

Last but not least, let's talk about soap. The best thing you can do for your skin is to wash it with a plain, nourishing, fragrance-free Dove bar. It cleans without significantly altering your natural body odor or skin biome. However, gentle nourishing shower gel can be used by men who need some extra scents to mask their natural odor. You can also choose your soap based on your skin type. There are options for people with dry, normal, or sensitive skin. Never use a two-in-one or, worse, a three-in-one product. A hair-washing product cannot possibly be beneficial to your face and body. It appears to save time and money, but it is harmful to your skin and hair in the long run. You should have two soaps, one for the body and one for the face. Your face wash should be tailored to your skin type as well. If your skin is naturally oily, look for an oil-controlling product. The same is true for oily or normal skin. There are also products available for those with sensitive skin. Any skin condition changes the scene from standing in a supermarket aisle to consulting your doctor. When you finish your shower or bath, depending on the weather, you can also moisturize your body. Skin can become extremely dry in both extremely hot and extremely cold climates. Winter, summer, and extremely hot showers all dry out your skin more. So, every few days, apply a body moisturizer, and your skin will feel and look better before you know it.

Nailing it.

Your nails are just as important to your overall appearance. Throughout the day, many people will look at your hands, and dirty hands can be a huge turn-off for both the ladies and the guys. The length of your nails isn't as important as the cleanliness of your nail beds. You can clean your nails by simply washing your hands, making it relatively simple to keep your nails clean. You can file or even buff your nails to make them look smooth and healthy if you want to go the extra mile. Nowadays, many men get their nails done as well. Matte clear nail polish protects your nails while also looking great. So, if you don't mind, you can do that on occasion. If not, there is no need to worry; simply clean your nails or invest in a nail brush for when you take a shower.

Clothing:

No one has the right to tell you how to present yourself, but if you're a man over the age of 18 and want to leave a positive impression, you have plenty of options at your disposal. To achieve that polished, expert appearance, consider some of the following alternatives.

A navy blue suit and/or a gray suit. In a suit, any man stands out. They are custom-made to highlight all of our best features. Gray and navy blue suits complement the majority of skin tones, hair colors, and eye colors. They are also distinct in their ability to demonstrate your style and individuality because they are not the traditional black.

A knitted tie, as well as other ties.
If you have suits, a nice tie or two is a must. A knitted tie is distinct in that it is finely knitted, adding an interesting texture to your suit ensemble. Other ties, such as satin ties, are also good for a shine and come in a variety of great color options.

A vest or two.
Vests can be worn with T-shirts for a dressier but casual look, and they add flair to formal outfits. They also sit quite tightly, giving the impression of a stronger, more defined chest or enhancing an already strong chest. Who wouldn't want to appear to have a nice chest? If you have gray or navy blue suits, the vests can be worn with the opposite suit for added depth.

A white and a blue dress shirt are a must in every man's arsenal.
Dress shirts exude sophistication. The white can go with both your navy blue and gray suits. To maintain the understated, classy look, pair the blue with your gray suit. For dressy occasions and work, pair them with nicer denim and chinos. People will take you seriously, and you may win prizes for being best-dressed.

A polo shirt.

A nice clean, ironed, collared polo shirt is no longer just for the golf course. They make anyone appear to have more money and maturity. They elevate your style from "bro" to "sir" when paired with a smart-looking watch and denim. Almost any color will work, but if you have darker skin or features, try some warmer colors like red, orange, or yellow. Cold, pastel colors work well if you have lighter features or a lighter skin tone. Light blue, green, and white are for such gentlemen. Black polo shirts with colored lines look great on everyone. Black is always a good color to wear because it is slimming. Remember that horizontal lines make you appear wider, while vertical lines make you appear taller. So horizontal lines are good for thinner men and vertical lines are good for heavier men who want to appear smaller.

A white, gray or black T-Shirt.

T-shirts come in a variety of styles, some with pictures or prints, some multicolored, and others plain. There are various cuts, such as V-necks and crew necks, and some people can pull off one or the other. V-neck T-shirts show off a more confident, outgoing personality and allow you to breathe more easily because they aren't as restrictive around your neck. Crew necks (the standard round-necked T-shirts) are for men who prefer a more casual, less statement-making look. You should purchase a white, gray, or black T-shirt because these colors go with everything and a white T-shirt is a classic. If you've seen the movies *Grease* or *Footloose*, you're familiar with the effect these have. Anyone can look good and clean in a pair of denim jeans and a white T-shirt. If you want a more playful look, get one with print displaying your fandoms, interests, or wit. These T-shirts also make excellent conversation starters. They can, however, make someone appear childish or younger. So keep that in mind when purchasing a printed T-shirt.

Jeans made of denim that age well.

Denim jeans will never go out of style, but the denim style may. Let me explain. Jeans are a great staple in any wardrobe, but various cuts go in and out of style as the years pass. It has even gotten to the point where your choice of jeans can reveal your age. Regular-fit jeans appear to be in style now and forever, but 90s babies prefer skinny jeans. Bootcut jeans are popular among cowboys and fans of 1970s fashion. Depending on your style, any denim will do. Remember that you can do more with whole jeans than with jeans with holes. The torn style is edgy and sexy, but it is mostly worn as casual clothing. If your jeans don't have holes or aren't torn on the knees or elsewhere, you can wear them to semi-formal events and even in the dead of winter. (Also, ripped jeans start looking bad on some people after a certain age, so keep this in mind as you get older.) The color of your denim can also reveal a lot about your personality. The darker, the edgier, and the lighter, the more boy-next-door. It's the distinction between a rocker and a "cool geek" look. Lighter jeans make you appear more sensitive and approachable.

Chinos.

Chinos are khaki or cream-colored pants that go with almost any outfit. They exude a sense of class and sophistication that many people admire. Particularly the person wearing them. Having a pair or two can significantly improve your overall mature appearance.

Black and brown belt.

Unless you practice a martial art, a black belt should always be worn with black shoes, and the same is true for a brown belt. Pair your suits and denim with a plain leather belt in either color or both. Because black looks better with gray, black belts frequently have a silver clasp or buckle. Brown belts go well with earth tones, and their clasps are frequently gold or brass in color. Brown belts go with chinos, denim, and suits, depending on whether you have matching brown shoes. Black is more formal, whereas brown can also be worn casually.

A sweater or two.

There are various types of sweaters. Cardigans are open sweaters with or without buttons that allow you to close them at the front like a dress shirt or hang them at your sides. Pullovers, also known as sweater vests, are sweaters that end at the shoulders and do not have sleeves. There are also V-neck and crew neck sweaters, as well as sweaters that zip up and others that only zip up from the mid-chest to the top. The traditional turtleneck sweater is another option. Rugby shirts and sweatshirts are hybrids of a sweater and a shirt. You can purchase any of these items from the store. They all contribute to a more fleshed-out appearance, whether you want to appear more professional, artistic, or simply cuddly. They are all comfortable and stylish.

Coats.

You have a plethora of options, just like with sweaters. Coats include everything from peacoats and parkas to windbreakers and puffer jackets. Longer coats make you appear more formal and professional, while shorter coats are ideal for outdoor activities and casual occasions. When it comes to your wardrobe, having one of each in a variety of styles is something to strive for.

A comfy hoodie.

Almost everyone has a cozy hoodie in their closet. It is very comfortable and casual, and it can be worn as part of a very stylish ensemble. When paired with a coat or a leather jacket, a nice pair of jeans, and sneakers, it creates the ideal look for a party or a date. You can get one that zips all the way up or one that doesn't and has a large pocket for both hands.

Accessories:

- **A stylish watch** is the age-old classic addition to any outfit. The more formal your watch is, the more metallic it is. There are numerous styles and sizes available for any occasion. Find something you like, but don't get too attached to it unless you adore the aesthetic. Get one for formal occasions and one for everyday wear. Of course, you can also opt for a smartwatch that can track your caloric intake, heart rate, and sleep pattern, and display your messages or answer your phone.

- **A scarf or two.**
They complete an outfit and provide warmth. Scarves can be worn with T-shirts for a different look, and they come in a variety of knits, materials, and wearing options (folding styles).

- **A few hats and caps** are ideal for sports and casual wear. Fedoras make a strong first impression. Knitted hats go well with scarves, and there are many other options. They are also reasonably priced.

- **Men's bracelets** have become increasingly available at trendy boutiques in recent years. They give you a youthful look. Beads in earth tones and a classy watch are the finishing touches on your ensembles that will have everyone talking. They make a bold, outgoing statement.

- **Necklaces, like bracelets and watches**, can convey a sense of individuality and creativity, and their designs can range from grungy and dark to dreamy and fantastical. Don't let outdated ideas about what men should wear prevent you from expressing yourself if you enjoy wearing a necklace.

- **Rings.**
In the past, there was symbolic significance associated with each finger on which a ring was worn. Today, however, it can just mean you have style and enjoy a stylish ring to tie your look together.

Cleaning is Purifying

How to Remove Most Stains

Pre-wash and specific stain remover sprays work very well on most stains, but some stains are more difficult to remove than others. Fortunately, many people have tested almost anything on stains over the years and discovered some surefire ways to combat the most difficult stains. Try these tried-and-true methods:

Type of stain: Grass

Product(s) needed: Toothpaste

An old toothbrush dipped in clean water and a dab of plain white toothpaste (paste, not gel) will do the trick. Use this method on all the stains, and then rinse and wash as usual.

Type of stain: Blood

Product(s) needed: Salt, baking soda, or hydrogen peroxide

You can do this in one of three ways. First, soak it in hydrogen peroxide, then use your fingernails or a butter knife to scrape off the blood. Finally, rinse it in more hydrogen peroxide. Wash and dry.

To use baking soda, leave it in a bowl of baking soda overnight before washing.

The third option is to use water and salt. The stain can be removed by rubbing its two ends together and then being washed.

Type of stain: Collar sweat stains

Product(s) needed: Shampoo

Pour some shampoo on it (oil-control shampoo is ideal, but regular shampoo will do). Next, you'll want to rub the ends together, soak it for 30 minutes, and then rinse it. After that just wash as normal.

Type of stain: Lipstick

Product(s) needed: Dish soap

Place it on some paper toweling stained side down, and rub some dish soap into the back of the stain. To clean it, flip it over and use a toothbrush. Machine wash on the gentle cycle, without rinsing. If the stain is still present, try the process again.

Type of stain: Grease

Product(s) needed: Cornstarch or WD-40 and dish soap

Use cornstarch to treat. Keep it there for a while, and then brush it off. The WD-40 method involves spraying the stain with the solvent and letting it sit for half an hour. Soak for another half an hour after adding dish soap. Launder it after.

Type of stain: Oil (cooking)

Product(s) needed: Salt and soda water

Soak the stain with salt, brush off the salt, and then treat it with club soda. If you are out and about and accidentally spill oil, this method is effective even in restaurants. (Note: if you get a stain and can't treat it at home, dab it instead of rubbing it.)

Type of stain: Oil (from your skin)

Product(s) needed: Shampoo, dish soap, or white chalk

Pour on some shampoo or dish soap, rub it in, let it sit for 15 minutes, then rinse it out and wash as usual. With chalk it is the same; just don't rinse it. Shake or brush it off and launder.

Type of stain: Ink

Product(s) needed: Use rubbing alcohol and cold water or ammonia, liquid detergent, and hot water.

There are two methods because there are two types of ink. Ink from ballpoint pens use the first and ink from felt-tip pens use the second. Put rubbing alcohol on the stain after putting it on a paper towel. Leave it for 15 minutes, then dab at the stain until the ink doesn't transfer anymore and finally rinse it and wash it in the machine. Rinse ink from a felt-tip pen with cold water, then soak it in hot water with a bit of detergent and ammonia after rubbing the stain under water. Leave it overnight, rub it with a bit more detergent and launder.

Type of stain: Red wine

Product(s) needed: Baking soda, salt, and boiling water

If the wine is wet pour over baking soda immediately and dab the stain gently. Stretch the stain over a big bowl and fasten it with a rubber band. Add salt over it and let it rest. Pour boiling water from 8 inches above the stain then launder it in hot water.

Type of stain: Tea

Product(s) needed: Cold water, detergent, or baking soda

Rinse it with cold water on the opposite side of the stain. Apply the detergent. Allow it to stand for 15 minutes. If it's already dried, repeat the process but wait 30 minutes. Rinse it once more and launder it. Baking soda is even simpler; simply pour it over the stain, brush it off, and wash your clothes.

(Hoyt, 2010)

How to Iron Your Clothes

You can speed up the process by placing aluminum foil on the ironing board beneath the fabric that is usually draped over it. This creates a heat barrier that repels heat from the bottom, so every time you iron, you "iron" the underside of your clothes as well.

Before you begin, make sure your iron is clean; a dirty iron can iron in new stains, rendering the entire process useless.

Make sure the clothes you want to iron are iron safe. On the tag, there should be a small iron symbol. If there isn't one, look at the materials used to make the clothes and do a quick internet search. This search should also show you which ironing setting to use. If not, the user manual definitely will tell you.

Set up your ironing board. If you don't have one make sure the area you are ironing on is not flammable.

If your iron has the option, add filtered water to the iron at the top so you can use the steam function. Turn on the iron and select the appropriate function from your research.

After you have laid the piece of clothing out flat and wrinkle-free, you can begin ironing. Begin at one end and work your way to the other using slow, even strokes. Alternatively, you can begin on the outsides, such as the sleeves, and work your way in (How to Iron Clothes - Step by Step, 2019).

Don't leave the iron in one spot for too long, and always put it down with the flat bit to the side and the base at the bottom. You can continue and then do the other side.

Keep hangers handy for your shirts, and when you're done, remember to let the iron cool before turning it off.

• • • ● ● • ● ● • •

Want to learn how to "dress to kill"? Check out this great course on style and fashion. Click on the link or scan the QR code below.

Dress to Kill: A Men's Primer on Style and Fashion

CHAPTER 6

HOW WILL YOU PAY FOR EVERYTHING?

H AVING A SOLID, WELL-PLANNED budget in place is the first step to taking control of your financial situation.

I've included a budget worksheet in the free bonus materials at *https://adultinghardbooks.com*.

- Add up the money you earn from all sources.

- Some of your income may be temporary, while other income may be consistent. Don't dwell on the temporary income, but figure it out anyway. For example, if you receive birthday money, consider it a one-time income and add it to your savings total that month, but don't consider it a monthly occurrence.

- Once you have your total, you can plan your monthly budget.

- Put together your non-negotiable expenses first and make sure you can cover those, such as rent, utilities, gas, and food.

- If you have automated debit orders, make sure they don't drain your bank account before you can cover these other expenses. Netflix is great, but it won't help you if you're homeless.

- The remainder can be divided between savings and non-essential purchases. Always save a little so you have a rainy-day fund or can afford something big later.

While having a budget is essential, it will be useless if you fail to follow it. In addition to prioritizing your needs over your wants, you should make having a savings plan a mandatory part of your life. This is the key to a secure financial future.

Do I Really Need an Xbox?

Although it's exciting to make large purchases, there are some things you should consider first:

- Do you have the money? Make certain that you do not deplete your savings or rainy-day fund. (A rainy-day fund is your emergency fund for unexpected large expenses. These would be considered hospital fees, car repair fees, and so on.)

- Is this a need or a want? Basic needs include things like clothing, food, shelter, safety, and social interaction, whereas wants include things like material possessions, entertainment, and other luxuries. However, some wants are more important to you than others. Some wants are also needs, but not in the sense that you need them to survive, but rather in the sense that you need them to carry out your duties or accomplish other objectives. Depending on whether they can help you succeed more effectively, define these for yourself and treat them as super important needs or wants.

- If I need it, do I need it now? For example, if you are an artist or art student, you might want the newest electronic drawing pad for digital art, but maybe not right now. However, having that electronic pad becomes mandatory when applying for a job at a company that specializes in digital artwork. For the time being, you can do without the drawing pad and showcase your hand-drawn work, but in a few months, you will require it. For those cases, it's smart to start putting money aside now. It all depends on the specifics of each situation.

- Are there cheaper, used, or good knock-offs available? This happens a lot with clothing items or furniture. An apple crate can serve as a coffee table. If you need new shoes and Air Jordans are your favorites, there may be shoes that look similar that are less expensive and look just as good. It fully depends on the alternatives. If this is a non-negotiable point, ask yourself the next question:

- When is it likely to go on sale? Most items go on sale at some point, and many items are cheaper directly from the supplier. So, if you really want the product, check to see if there is an upcoming store sale or if the supplier can quote you a lower price *(Caldwell, 2021)*.

Making the Most of Your Money

Sometimes you have to cut expenses to make ends meet or to make saving for large purchases easier.

- To do so, you should track all of your spending habits, create and stick to a budget, and ensure that your subscriptions and/or debit orders are still frequently used and not draining all of your money.

- Aside from that, you can try to save in small ways every day, such as saving electricity; if you don't have a roommate, you might want to reconsider that decision; if you have a paid parking space, you could get rid of it; and if you buy daily items, such as coffee, you could get a smaller size or bring some from home.

- If you have debt, you can consolidate it by combining all of your payments into one.

- You can also lower your insurance costs.

- You can start eating at home or stay in when everyone goes out partying, here and there.

- When you go shopping, stick to your list and try not to stray; this will help you save money gradually until your finances shine.

- You can either stop using your credit cards or completely freeze them. When you pay with cash, you can see exactly how much you spend, so try to do so as much as possible *(Milliken, 2022)*.

Investing in Your Future:

When you become more financially stable, or even when things begin to look up, a good investment can ensure that you are cared for, for a long time.

You have the best resource for investing as a young person: time. If you are in your twenties, you have 40 years before retirement, so think about how much money you can save up until then. Your savings should be geared toward long-term growth. Consider investing some or all of your savings (other than your rainy-day fund) in common stocks or other equities. Another option is to invest in a mutual fund that invests in real estate holdings. This is known as a REIT. The important thing is to make as much money as possible while you are still young enough to work.

When you join the workforce they usually have a pension plan in a lot of countries. Only a small number of U.S. companies offer them today, however. If you can find one in the U.S., or if you work elsewhere, the company will match your contributions, meaning that when you retire, you will have double the pension you had before (Cussen, 2022).

You can learn more about how to make a budget by checking out this course. Just click on the link or scan the QR code below.

*Learn How To Budget for
Teens and Young Adults*

CHAPTER 7

LOOK OUT!

D ISASTERS CAN STRIKE AT any time. Being smart can help you prepare for these and other dangerous situations. This chapter will provide you with information on how to deal with natural disasters, ideas for how to deal with scammers and the scams they use to catch you, and some first aid options if the worst happens.

Natural Disaster Preparations

Understanding the risks is the first step in any disaster. It all depends on where you live. Earthquakes do not occur naturally in Africa, for example, because the continent is on the African tectonic plate, but people in North America, particularly in the west, may experience earthquakes due to their location on the San Andreas fault. Conduct some research to determine which natural disasters, if any, are common in your area.

Make an emergency plan. You need to put together steps for evacuation. Know where you need to go. Because you might not have power during a disaster, you might want to get the information and make a plan before it happens. Know where the evacuation centers are and, if there aren't any, where the safest places are for the natural disasters that could happen in your area. Also, it's a good idea to get a radio that can work in all kinds of weather and has batteries in case of an emergency.

If you have pets, you should make sure they have carriers, and if they need medicine, you should get enough for a week.

When you make your plan, you can start to think about how to get your home and car ready in case something goes wrong. Most people put together "bug-out bags" with extra clothes, canned food, a pillow, blankets or a sleeping bag, flares, matches, a lot of water, flashlights and first-aid kits, extra batteries, wet wipes, plastic bags, pet food, and anything else they can think of.

A can of pepper spray might be a good idea because some people get violent when they are scared, and others use that as an opportunity to break into places. If you take any medicine, remember to think more about that as well.

One of these bags should be in your car and the other should be in your house. There are also a lot of camping supplies that can help if you're worried you might get stuck somewhere. Some of these things are water purification tablets, a pocket knife, a camping shower, and anything else you see in a camping store that you think might be useful.

You can also get ready by securing your outdoor furniture and buying sandbags if you think some parts of your house might flood.

Then it would be smart to know where your entrances and utility shut-offs are. You can also keep your faucets from freezing by leaving them a little bit open so the water is running in the pipes.

You can waterproof your windows and doors and think about getting a portable power bank, or battery, which you can find at most hardware stores. You might also feel better with a power bank for your phone.

Before a natural disaster, you can make sure your car is in proper working order and prepared by taking it to a mechanic for any preparations applicable to the type of disaster.

When everything is ready, you can make a list to make sure you have everything and practice your survival plan. Remember that the best way to stay alive is to be ready for anything (Jackery team, 2022).

• • • ● • ● • • •

Scammers Scram!

Someone trying to trick you is another danger that can happen at any time. Most people don't realize how often it happens, and it can cost you everything from your hard-earned money to your identity.

Watch out for the following:

- If they get in touch with you first, rather than you contacting them, they might be setting up a scam. This is a classic case of stranger danger. If you contact a business first, you know whom you are talking to, but if they contact you, they could be making up their email address or phone number. Always assume the person contacting you might not be who they say they are.

As Joseph Heller wrote in *Catch 22*: *"Just because you're paranoid doesn't mean they aren't after you."*

- If they promise you free money or free anything, beware. People don't give away money and nothing in life is free. If they promise things that seem too good to be true they usually are. Take any situation like that with a grain of salt.

- If they want information about you. As part of their phone call scripts, many businesses can't ask people for their personal information because it's against the law. If someone asks for your social security number, ID number, or contact information, they could be trying to steal your identity.

- If you have to pay them before you can get certain benefits, or if you have to pay for something, like a prize or something else, it could be a scam. A good rule is to only pay someone after they have done something for you or when you buy something from them in person. Most of the time, you don't have to interact with people when you shop online, but once again, that interaction starts with you.

- Don't send gift cards or wire money for prizes or to pay off debts. To pay your debts, you would get a letter or multiple letters, and people would talk to you in person, or you could take their information and make sure they are whom they say they are first. Never just pay unless you know exactly what you're paying for and have an account with them.

- Don't trust them if they won't let you check any of their information over the phone. Also, watch out for people on dating sites who want money from you. You shouldn't have to pay for a date with someone you haven't even seen yet (Common Scams | Office of the Attorney General, n.d.).

• • ● ● ● • ● ● ● •

Playing Doctor

This section is split into three parts: common ways to stay safe around the house, things that should be in every first-aid kit, and how to give first aid and know when to go to the doctor. Please keep in mind that I'm not a doctor, but there are links to other sources, and if you're ever not sure what to do in an emergency, it's best to call an ambulance.

Common Ways to Avoid Accidents and Injuries at Home:

- **Keep your rugs flat and where they belong.** You can put rubber pads on the bottom of rugs that don't move, or you can use double-sided tape to keep rugs in place. This makes sure that nobody trips and falls.

- **Non-slip mats** should also be used in bathrooms and showers to keep people safe. Many hard, slippery surfaces in the bathroom could seriously hurt you or your guests. You should also make sure that your railings and handles are securely fastened so that if you do slip, you can catch yourself and not fall.

- **Make sure there's enough light.** When you can't see what's around you and you have to move quickly for any reason, you're in a dangerous situation. An injury-free home begins with adequate lighting.

- **Try to keep the floor as clear as possible.** If there is nothing to trip over, then injuries from tripping are less likely—unless you forget to tie your shoelaces, but I can't help you with that. Also, a clean house makes it less likely that you'll get an infection if you have an accident.

- **Make sure your cables are out of the way and hidden.** Cables can get tangled and messy, which not only looks bad but could also be dangerous. If you can find a way to hide them behind something, do so.

- **Clean up any spills right away.** If the floor is wet, you or someone else who doesn't know about it could slip and hit something on the way down. Before that happens, it's best to clean up.

- **Hot liquids should be stored in a safe place.** Liquids in general, but especially hot ones, should be placed closer to the center of a table rather than the edges. You can also keep liquids far away from any technology since a short circuit from wet technology can send sparks flying and start a fire.

- **Make sure your water heater** isn't hotter than 120 degrees Fahrenheit (48 degrees Celsius) because anything hotter than that can burn someone in the shower.

- **Don't leave any tools or utensils lying around.** Accidents happen, but if you put away dangerous items, you can limit the damage to yourself, other people, and the house. This is especially true for powered tools.

- **Don't keep cleaning supplies** where pets, kids, or anyone else could trip over them or ingest them. Most cleaning supplies are poisonous if eaten, and things like mops and buckets are the easiest to knock over. Having a safe space for them saves everyone a trip to the doctor.

- **Disconnect anything you're not using.** Many things can start a fire, but nothing is as common as a short from frayed wires or a broken plug. Make sure these aren't plugged in when you're not there or at least turn the switch off as often as you can.

- **Use surge protectors** on all of your extension cords. When you don't have anything plugged in, these switches stop any electricity from going through.

- **Don't leave cooking or flames unattended** for more than a few seconds. Also, keep anything that can catch fire away from the stove or oven. If you ever have a grease fire, DO NOT try to put it out with water or a wet towel, because that will make things a lot worse.

- **Don't smoke in the house**, even if you or someone else does. When you smoke cigarettes or anything else, the ash can fall off and start a fire. Outside, there are a lot more things that won't catch fire and a lot more ways to put them out.

- **Make sure to take the lint out of the dryer** and clean the filters on other machines. All of these are dangerous if left alone for too long. When clothes are in the dryer and the lint is moving around, it creates static and sparks. It also gets very hot, and if the heat has nowhere to go, it can start a fire in the lint.

- **When you leave the house, turn off any appliances** or blow out any candles. If you like to burn incense or candles, put them out before you leave, even if you're only going to be gone for a short time. The same is true for anything else that heats up before you leave, like a toaster, oven, or heater.

The following resources can be used to learn more about these tips: (Console Jr., 2021) (How to Prevent the Most Common Household Accident, n.d.) (How to Prevent Fire in Your Home, 2018).

As a bonus safety tip, you should make it a top priority to get a fire extinguisher. They are around $30 USD, and they have simple instructions on how to use them.

Items every first-aid kit needs:

- Band-aids

- Bandages

- Alcohol wipes

- Adhesive

- Antibiotic ointment

- Gauze

- Hand sanitizer

- Latex-free gloves

- Painkillers

- Scissors and tweezers

- Q-tips

- Antiseptic spray

- Aloe vera cream

- Cotton swabs

- Syringes

- Cold packs

- Calamine lotion

- Saline wound wash

- Anything else you find at the pharmacy that might help

How to handle an emergency and when to call for help:

- Cuts and scrapes

  - Wash your hands and use pressure and gauze to stop any bleeding. Clean the wound with gauze and saline wound wash. If there is anything stuck in the wound, use tweezers to pull it out. If the wound is in a place where it might get dirty or irritated, put a bandage on it. When the scab forms, take off the bandage.

  - If the cut is too long or too deep, call a doctor or go to the ER. Also, if the edges are sharp. That means you might need a tetanus shot and/or stitches.

  - You should also go to the doctor if the cut was caused by a bite from an animal or person or by rusty metal.

- If you can't stop the bleeding with the pressure, you should see a doctor.

- Go to the hospital if the cut can't be cleaned and pus comes out of it, as you might need antibiotics.

- Seek medical attention if the skin around the wound becomes red and swollen, or if there are red streaks, or if you develop a fever.

- See a doctor if it's near a joint or on your face.

- Nosebleeds

  - Tilt your head forward, not back, to stop blood from going down your throat.

  - Use a tissue or washcloth to gently stop the bleeding.

  - Wait five to ten minutes and check to see if the bleeding has stopped.

  - Call the doctor if the bleeding hasn't stopped after 20 minutes or if there is a lot of blood flowing quickly.

  - Call the doctor if the bleeding is caused by an injury.

  - If you're feeling weak and dizzy, call the doctor.

- Splinters

  - Wash the area first, and then use alcohol to clean your tweezers.

  - Grab the splinter by the end and pull it out at the same angle it went in.

  - Clean the area again.

  - If the splinter doesn't have a sharp edge sticking out, you also need an alcohol-cleaned needle to scrape the skin open a bit before doing the steps above. If you don't have alcohol, you can sterilize the tip with the flame from a lighter. Just let it cool down before you use it.

- Animal or insect bites and stings

- ○ For animal bites, use a towel or gauze to stop the bleeding, soap, and water to clean the wound, and a bandage to cover it. Then you should go to the doctor because any bite from an animal needs antibiotic treatment and might need a rabies shot. If the bite is big, apply pressure to the wound and go to the doctor right away.

- ○ If you've been stung by an insect, make sure the stinger is gone or scrape it off with something flat and dull, like a credit card. Then wash it and cool it to stop the swelling. Use calamine lotion to take care of the pain. If you get hives, feel dizzy, have cramps, vomit, have trouble breathing, or your tongue swells up, you should go to the emergency room right away. If you know you have an allergy, you should keep an epinephrine auto-injector pen at home.

- ○ If it's a spider bite, watch out for red or purple skin around the bite, a lot of pain, swelling, a rash, muscle pain, a fever, chills, stomach pain, nausea and vomiting, and trouble breathing. If you have any of these, you should see a doctor right away.

- • Minor burns

  - ○ First-degree burns are red and may swell, second-degree burns form blisters and are very painful, and third-degree burns turn white or look scorched and may not hurt at all because nerves may have been damaged.

  - ○ You should see a doctor if you have third-degree burns. If the burn is big or on your joints, hands, feet, or face, you should also go to the doctor. If the pain keeps getting worse instead of better, you should also go. You should go to the emergency room if there is pus or if the burn was caused by chemicals or electricity.

  - ○ To treat a minor burn keep it under cold running water for the swelling, get an antiseptic spray or aloe cream to soothe it then wrap it loosely with bandages or gauze.

If you don't know how to treat other injuries, you can go to the doctor or look at www.webmd.com site (Watson, 2015).

If you're looking for a complete basic course on first aid, click on this link or scan the QR code below.

*First Aid Masterclass: A
Complete Guide to First
Aid*

CHAPTER 8

STAY HAPPY AND ALIVE!

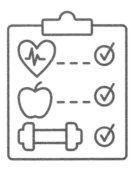

WHEN YOU LIVE BY yourself, it's easy to feel a little down and depressed. Everyone's mind is unique, and different things excite different people in different ways. Some healthy habits can improve your health as a whole:

I have included a habit tracker to help you build and integrate healthy habits into your life. You can find it as part of the bonus materials at https://adultinghardbooks.com.

Consider following any and all of the following healthy habits.

- **Fall into good sleeping habits.** That means getting enough sleep without oversleeping or sleeping too little every night. People who don't get enough sleep tend to die younger too.

- **If you're feeling down** or need a pick-me-up, get some fresh air and go outside.

Natural light and air are known to improve one's mood.

- **Practice safe sex.** Unsafe sex can cause a slew of concerns and problems. Pregnancy or STIs are always a risk factor, and the stress of the possibility of either can cause emotional distress in anyone.

- **Wear sunscreen.** Sunscreen is beneficial for both moisturizing and preventing sunburn and skin cancer.

- **Do not smoke.** If you don't quit smoking before the age of 30, you could lose up to ten years of your life. Smoking poses numerous health risks and makes you appear not only physically unhealthy but also like a loser. As a smoker, your skin, eyes, and teeth all look worse. Which is detrimental to your self-esteem.

- **Make your meals and try to eat out less.** If you can control the ingredients and portions of your food, you can live a longer and healthier life.

- **Eat a variety of colors of fruits and vegetables.** They are extremely beneficial to your cardiovascular health.

- **Cut out sugar, especially soda.** The number of health problems associated with eating too much sugar is staggering. Sugary foods and drinks, just like cigarettes, should be avoided.

- **Drink plenty of water.** At least eight glasses per day. Water is an essential component of all living things on the planet. It is a basic requirement, and getting enough of it benefits your skin, all of your organs, your muscles, and other body functions. Get a glass of water whenever you are thirsty or simply because you are sitting idle or working. I guarantee that you'll be better off as a result.

- **Stand up and stretch now and then.** Sitting all day can be harmful for a variety of reasons; try to get up and move around. If you've been sitting for a while, get up and move around for 10 minutes. The more time you spend sitting, the more walking and staying active you need to do. So, if you have to sit for a long time, try to do what you need to do while standing, dancing, or doing anything other than sitting or lying down.

- **Express gratitude.** Research shows that grateful people also live longer.

- **Don't drink too much.** If you drink, don't drink too much. Alcohol is also a depressant, so too much of it can make you feel worse.

- **Have plenty of intercourse.** Sex is good for your heart, it makes you feel good by releasing endorphins, it helps with headaches and migraines, and it makes your immune system stronger. If you don't have a partner to have sex with, try to ejaculate at least once a day on your own. Yes! Among the benefits of ejaculating regularly are:

    - Lowering the risk of prostate cancer

    - Helps with incontinence and erectile dysfunction

    - Helps you last longer during sex

    - Boosts immunity

    - Improves your mood (as long as you are not a sex addict)

    - Helps you sleep at night

    - Can add years to your life

    - It's good for your heart

(Reyes & Matthews, 2016)

- **Stay away from toxic people.** You don't want anyone in your life who makes you feel like you're not a legend and who only cares about themselves. You should hang out with people you can trust to keep your biggest secrets and help you through hard times. The best friend is someone who lets you be vulnerable, but who can also challenge your worldview and give you something to think about. Go out with them and try to talk to them about something small. See how they react, and by the end of the night, see if they look out for their friends instead of ditching a man for something else.

- **Have regular dental and medical checkups.** Doctors can make sure you don't have any problems, which will take one worry off your plate. In your 20s, your body stops changing as quickly and dramatically as it did in your teens. Having a clean bill of health or knowing where you need to make changes in your life can also do a lot for your mental health.

Meditate

Meditation is another way to relieve stress and calm down.

One great technique is to work on the seven chakra systems; it helps you take stock of every part of your life. It is simple and easy to fit into your schedule because you can do it for any length of time (Stelter, 2016).

Just learn about the different chakras.

- Close your eyes and think of the color of the chakra as a light that gets brighter and dimmer as you breathe.

- Focus on what that color means. For example, to start with the root chakra, close your eyes and picture a red light pulsing as you take slow, deep breaths. This chakra is about how safe you feel, so think about all the things in your life, and right now that makes you feel safe.

- You can move on to the next chakra when you feel calm doing the things that make you feel safe. It's simple and easy to do (Kylstra, 2014).

If thinking about chakras is too much for you, all you need to do to meditate is sit still for a few minutes and pay attention to your breath and everything around you. Meditation can help you even if you don't lock yourself in a Buddhist temple.

If Boys Can Cry So Can Men

One of the worst things about being a man at any time in history is the idea that after we grow up, we shouldn't feel or show how we feel, especially if those feelings are sadness, happiness, or anger, which are the big three.

What happens, though, when pressure builds up in a sealed container? It goes off with a loud bang that can hurt anyone nearby, and then the container is all broken up.

Don't let that container be you.

When you have strong feelings, don't bottle them up. Instead, deal with them as they come up. I'm not saying that you should hit something when you're mad, though.

There are different ways to express anger, sadness, and happiness. First, you have to be able to recognize the right feelings.

The Feelings Wheel

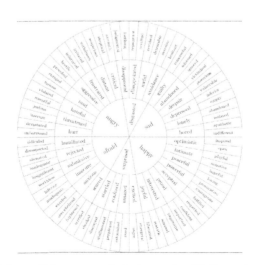

Dr. Robert Plutchik, a well-known psychologist, made a "feelings wheel" to help people understand how they feel. It shows the full range of human feelings, from the strongest to the weakest (Cooks and Campbell, 2022). This wheel helps you learn more about yourself and shows you which emotions are the opposites of each other. This is good because if you meet someone with the opposite emotion, it can make yours worse or you might fight them. Look at the source or do your own research to figure out what's going on with your feelings.

CBT

You can also try CBT (Cognitive Behavioral Therapy). This method of self-analysis and mental health care has been tested and proven by science. It helps you find limiting thoughts and mental distortions that affect how you feel and, as a result, how you act.

These limiting thoughts include:

- **All-or-nothing or polarized thinking** — seeing everything as either bad or good, with no middle ground

- **Catastrophizing** — thinking the worst will happen

- **Shoulds** — Having arbitrary rules for how you and others should act.

- **Magnification and minimization** — Making problems seem bigger and good things seem less important.

- **Selective abstraction or filtering** — Focusing on the negative while filtering out the positive

- **Mind reading** — assuming you know what others are thinking and feeling

- **Overgeneralization** — making sweeping statements based on scanty evidence

- **Personalization** — assuming the reactions of others always relate to you

If you like what you read about this process, you can speak with a psychologist who is familiar with it (American Psychological Association, 2017).

I made a very helpful worksheet to help you find any limiting beliefs that might be getting in the way of you processing your feelings and actions in a healthy way and work through them.

I use it all the time, and it has helped me a lot (yes, even adults my age deal with anxiety and limiting thoughts and beliefs). You can find it at *https://adultinghardbooks.com*.

If you have severe anxiety or only a mild form of anxiety, you can concentrate on breathing techniques such as one found on the NHS website in the United Kingdom (NHS, 2021).

It entails finding a spot where you can practice your breathing every day. It can happen anywhere and in any shape or form, but if you're sitting, make sure you have lumbar support.

1. Remove or loosen any clothing that is restricting your breathing.

2. Keeping your legs shoulder-width apart, take a comfortable breath, counting from one to give, then slowly exhale on the same count.

3. Do this for five minutes, and you're done. If you have severe anxiety, you should know that you may have a panic attack depending on what sets it off.

This breathing technique will help you. You should also inform those around you that if you have a panic attack, they should hug you tightly and use this breathing technique in a calm voice.

There are numerous other ways to cope with your mental health; you simply need to look for them and, if necessary, consult a good psychologist. Their entire job is to assist you.

Attachment Styles: The Invisible Strings That Connect Us

As we embark on this journey of adulting, one of the most significant areas we encounter is building and managing relationships. Whether it's with friends, colleagues, or romantic partners, understanding your own and others' attachment styles can make a significant difference in how your relationships unfold.

Attachment styles are patterns of how we think, feel, and behave in relationships, which we develop based on our early interactions with caregivers. There are four primary attachment styles: Secure, Anxious, Avoidant, and Fearful-Avoidant.

1. Secure Attachment

Securely attached individuals tend to have a positive view of themselves and others. They feel comfortable with intimacy and are not usually worried about being alone or being rejected. In short, they're the relationship rock stars. They communicate their needs effectively, offer support when it's needed, and are comfortable seeking support when they need it.

2. Anxious Attachment

People with an anxious attachment style often worry about their partner's commitment and love. They tend to be "clingy" and may require constant reassurance. Think of them as the ones who double, triple, or quadruple text and fret when a reply doesn't come fast enough. They crave closeness and intimacy but often feel that their needs aren't being met.

3. Avoidant Attachment

Avoidant individuals value their independence to a great extent. They might seem like lone wolves, preferring to keep others at a distance and suppressing their feelings. They're the ones who might "ghost" you, sidestep commitment, or pull away when things start getting serious. Their motto is likely to be "I stand alone."

4. Fearful-Avoidant Attachment

This style is a mix of anxious and avoidant behaviors. Fearful-avoidant individuals have a hard time trusting and relying on others, and they often fear getting too emotionally involved. They want to have emotionally close relationships, but they find it hard to trust their partners or don't feel worthy of being loved.

Understanding and Adapting

Recognizing your own attachment style and understanding the styles of others can dramatically improve your relationships. Secure attachment is the goal, but don't worry if you don't quite fit that mold. Our attachment styles can change over time and with consistent effort.

For example, if you're anxiously attached, learning to self-soothe and provide self-reassurance can help reduce the need for constant validation. If you're avoidant, practicing vulnerability and allowing others to offer support can build trust and connection.

Remember, knowledge of attachment styles is not about labeling or blaming, but about understanding and adapting. As we continue to grow and "adult", developing secure attachments is just another part of the journey.

Get the Right Kind of Help

The world of health insurance can be difficult to navigate. Let's look at how health care is covered in different places around the world.

U.S. Health Insurance:

Health care in the United States can be very pricey. A single visit to the doctor's office can cost hundreds of dollars, while a three-day hospital stay can cost tens of thousands of dollars or even more, depending on the type of care given.

The consumer (you) usually pays an upfront premium to a health insurance company. This payment lets you share "risk" with a large number of other people (enrollees) who are also making similar payments. Most people are generally healthy, so the money paid to the insurance company in premiums can be used to pay for the costs of the (relatively few) people who get sick or hurt. As you might expect, insurance companies have done a lot of research on risk, and their goal is to get enough money from premiums to cover the medical costs of the people who sign up. In the U.S., there are many different kinds of health insurance plans, each with its own rules and care arrangements.

When looking for health insurance in the US, ask these three questions:

- Where can I go to receive care?

- What is covered under my plan?

- How much will it cost?

Terms that you should know:

- **Out-of-pocket expenses:** this is money you pay that isn't part of the premium when you visit the hospital. This is money that you pay out of your own pocket.

- **Annual deductible:** This is the amount you agreed to pay to the hospitals before your insurance kicks in. So if you have to pay an annual deductible of $2,000, the first two grand come out of your bank account, and after that, your insurance kicks in and pays a percentage of the rest. Yes, I said "a percentage." What? Did you think you were off the hook? Ha! Dream on!

- **Copayment or copay:** Each time you go to the doctor, you pay a smaller amount, which is similar to the annual deductible. You pay, let's say, $20, and if the doctor's visit costs more than that, the insurance company pays the rest. The more you pay in premiums (monthly payments), the less your copay will usually be.

- **Coinsurance** is the share of the cost of medical care that you pay for as part of your insurance agreement. For instance, if you get a CT scan, they will pay 80% of the cost and you will pay the other 20%. This is the percentage I mentioned in the section on the annual deductible.

- **Annual out-of-pocket maximum.** This is the most you will pay for your share of costs in a year. The sum of your deductible, copayment, and coinsurance for the year, but not your premium. After this amount, the insurance will cover everything else *(How U.S. Health Insurance Works | Vaden Health Services, n.d.).*

Canadian Health Insurance:

Canada has a universal health care system that is based on the territory or province you live in. This means that when you go to the hospital, the taxes you pay cover some things.

Workplace benefits and personal health and dental insurance are the other two kinds of insurance they have.

Universal health care usually covers:

- doctor's visits for the family, emergency room visits, outpatient clinic appointments

- inpatient care or surgery

- medicines as part of inpatient care

- diagnostic tests

- radiation therapy

- medicines in an outpatient care capacity like chemotherapy

- cancer support services

- mental health services

- prescription drugs

Workplace benefits are also offered by the company you work for. The fees are paid for by all the people who work for the company, so it is cheaper. These plans are also customizable. They usually cover:

- other prescription drugs not covered by the universal healthcare

- dental care

- vision care

- paramedical services

- ambulance services

The last type, personal health and dental insurance, is for retirees and people who are self-employed. It's basically the same as benefits at work, and you can get them even if you already have a pre-existing health condition. Usually, it includes:

- the same things as workplace benefits

- medical supplies

- hearing aids

- in-home nursing and care

- emergency travel medical

- major dental care

- accidental death and dismemberment

- hospital accommodation

So, most people in Canada don't get other kinds of health insurance, but some still do, just in case their other kinds of health care don't cover the bigger health problems (Health Insurance 101: How Does Health Insurance Work in Canada?, n.d.).

UK Health Insurance:

Permanent residents in the UK have access to the National Health Services (NHS). This is a lot like Canada's health care system, but it covers more people. Since everything is free, most people don't get health insurance. Since everyone pays taxes, you don't have to pay to go to the doctor. Consumers do pay for their prescription drugs, but it's always the same amount: nine pounds. Private companies and charities are also involved, but the government, specifically the health department, is in charge of most of the work.

If you are not a citizen of the UK and don't have indefinite leave to stay, you usually have to pay a health surcharge of between 150 and 200 pounds for every year you stay, depending on the type of visa you apply for. This fee is not required for all visas, though. Some people do get private health insurance so they can see specialists, wait less, and have better facilities (Buswell, 2014). People pay for dental care because it's not covered by the NHS, but it's not that expensive, so most people don't need insurance for it.

Australian Health Insurance:

Australia has a healthcare system called Medicare that covers everyone. It doesn't cover as much as the NHS in the UK or Canada's health care benefits. You can join Medicare and get a card that covers:

- seeing a GP (General Practitioner) or a specialist

- tests and scans

- most types of surgery

- eye exams

Medicare doesn't cover:

- ambulance

- dental services

- anything you might need after an eye exam or hearing test

- cosmetic surgery

Most people in Australia have private health insurance, but some places choose to use Medicare's bulk billing instead. That means a doctor can choose whether they want to be paid by their patients or by Medicare. Medicare doesn't cover everything, though, so it's more of a gamble if you don't know exactly what's covered. One type of private health insurance covers hospital stays and surgery costs, while the other covers general treatments like physiotherapy and dental care. When you have private health insurance, you can choose your own specialist and surgeon. You can also go to private hospitals or be admitted as a private patient in a public hospital. Health insurance costs vary from person to person, and the government sometimes gives money back to people who don't make a lot of money. It can be a little confusing, so if you want more information you can visit the Australian government's website about their health insurance https://www.health.gov.au (Health, 2019).

• • • ● ● • ● ● • •

If you want to learn more about Cognitive Behavioral Therapy (CBT) and how it can help you deal with social anxiety, check out this course by clicking on this link or scanning the QR code below.

Overcome Social
Anxiety using Cognitive
Behavioral Therapy

CHAPTER 9

THE MOST INTERESTING MAN IN THE WORLD

THIS CHAPTER WILL TALK about how to become a real Renaissance man. People tend to like a man who can have interesting conversations about travel, pop culture, and other things. With the information in this chapter, you can impress potential love interests and their parents, or simply make a few new interesting friends.

I've included a few checklists, bucket lists, and journaling sheets as free bonus materials to help you become a Renaissance Man. You can find them at *https://adultinghardbooks.com*

The following chart lists movies, series, and books all young men should consider.

Movies

Boyhood

Terminator II: Judgment Day

Fight Club

The Godfather

This is Spinal Tap

12 Years a Slave

Unforgiven

The Way Way Back

Saving Private Ryan

The Big Lebowski

Dr. Strangelove

Taxi Driver

Boyz N The Hood

The Raid

There Will Be Blood

All Is Lost

Straw Dogs

American Psycho

Frozen

The Shawshank Redemption

Raging Bull

Apocalypse Now

To Kill A Mockingbird

The Social Network

Citizen Kane

Pulp Fiction

Rebel With A Cause

Gladiator

Dead Poets Society

Moonlight

(Cooper, n.d.)

• • • ● ● • ● ● • •

TV Series

Mad Men

Sherlock

Suits

Downton Abbey

Archer

Peaky Blinders

Miami Vice

Boston Legal

Lucifer

How I Met Your Mother

White Collar

30 Rock

Luther

White Gold

Dexter

Hannibal

The Kominsky Method

Psych

Boardwalk Empire

Mr. Selfridge

Californication

Billions

Justified

The Marvelous Mrs. Maisel

Only Fools And Horses

The Boys

House of Cards

True Detective

Sons of Anarchy

Ozark

This Time With Alan Partridge

The Haunting of Hill House

(30+ Stylish TV Shows Every Man Should Binge, 2022)

Books

Less Than Zero - Brett Easton Ellis

Me Talk Pretty One Day - David Sedaris

A House for Mr. Biswas - V.S. Naipaul

Norwegian Wood - Haruki Murakami

One Flew Over The Cuckoo's Nest - Ken Kesey

Americanah - Chimamanda Ngozi Adichie

The Picture Of Dorian Grey - Oscar Wilde

The Love Song Of J. Alfred Prufrock - T. S. Eliot

The Satanic Verses - Salman Rushdie

The Secret History - Donna Tartt

Slaughterhouse Five - Kurt Vonnegut

The Brief Wondrous Life of Oscar Wao - Junot Díaz

The Fall - Albert Camus

My Struggle - Karl Ove Knausgaard

The Golden Notebook - Doris Lessing

The Road - Cormac McCarthy

What We Talk About When We Talk About Love - Raymond Carver

Generation X - Douglas Coupland

The Great Gatsby - F. Scott Fitzgerald

The Bell Jar - Sylvia Plath

On The Road - Jack Kerouac

White Teeth - Zadie Smith

Brave New World - Aldous Huxley

American Pastoral - Philip Roth

High Windows - Philip Larkin

Fear And Loathing In Las Vegas - Hunters S. Thompson

The Line Of Beauty – Alan Hollinghurst

The Catcher In The Rye - J D Salinger

Men Without Women - Ernest Hemingway

1984 - George Orwell

(30 Books Every Man Should Read by 30, 2020)

A Fact-Finding Mission

The Ten Best Places to Visit in the World:

What are the top ten places to travel to? This is like asking a parent, "Who is your favorite child?"

The list below is by no means exhaustive or objective. You might concur or disagree, depending on your personal preferences and tastes. But, you cannot dispute that the following locations are incredible places to visit, even though they might not rank among your personal "Top Ten" lists:

1. South Island, New Zealand

2. Paris

3. Maui

4. Bora Bora

5. Tahiti

6. London

7. Rome

8. Turks & Caicos

9. Tokyo

10. Maldives

(U.S. News, 2019)

Travel hacks:

1. Pack smart to make sure you save space in your luggage. Rolling your clothes is a great way to keep them wrinkle-free and well organized.

2. Add "fragile" to the tags on your bags.

3. Get around town even if you don't have service by downloading the offline maps of your destinations on Google Maps.

4. A credit card is your best way to pay abroad. Call ahead to let them know you will be traveling (even domestically), so you don't get blocked by their anti-fraud system.

5. Try to use apps for free calling on Wi-Fi as much as you can.

6. Drink filtered water at all times.

7. Wherever you go your documents need to be with you.

8. Make sure all of your devices are charged. You can also charge them via the hotel TV using a USB charger. Better yet, buy a universal travel adapter. They cost about $20, and you can use them to connect multiple USBs and other devices. I never travel without it, especially if there is only one outlet next to the bed and I need to charge my phone, watch, and earbuds.

9. Take a physical and digital copy of your passport with you. Make copies of your important documents and email them to yourself in case you lose your phone and need to access them online.

10. Remember to pack your first aid kit.

11. Put your rechargeable batteries in the fridge. The majority of electronics perform better in colder temperatures. In the fridge, they gain 90% of their full charge.

12. Remember your extension cable. Not all hotels have one, and in hostels, people fight to charge their devices. This will make sure your devices and possibly your friends' can get the charge they need.

13. If you go to a foreign country with a different language than yours, download Google Translate. Most people would be more inclined to help you if they understood what you wanted.

14. Use an ATM instead of the money exchange services at the airport. They charge extra fees and misuse the exchange rates. Rather, just use an ATM with your Visa or Mastercard.

15. Travel in shoulder seasons, i.e., September–November and March–May. This is between the low and high seasons. The weather is great, and the rates are more affordable.

16. Get a frequent flyer account with every airline you support. You gain points for your next trip, and this adds extra discounts on your future holidays.

17. Use a different "home" country when you book your flights. You can save if there is a better exchange rate.

18. Call the hotel instead of booking online. They can upgrade your accommodations, and you don't pay online booking fees.

19. Remember a universal adapter. Different countries use different plugs, but if you have an adapter, you can always charge your much-needed devices.

20. Consider buying a transport pass for the different forms of public transport, like the metro, trolley, etc. You can get everywhere you need to go, and you avoid waiting in lines daily.

(10 Travel Hacks You Must Know About, 2022, Menon, 2021)

Write it Out

Journaling is a good way to remember new facts and information you learn and to share your own thoughts about everything in your life. There are also many benefits for both your mental and physical health. It helps you deal with anxiety and depression, improves your memory, and can make a big difference in how much stress you feel. This is because it makes you feel better about your fears, breaks down your problems, and splits up your worries. It also keeps track of your symptoms so you can learn about your stressors and either stops you from thinking negative thoughts or gets them out.

How journaling works:

- You can keep a journal using apps or the old-fashioned way, with a pen and paper. Find a method you like and try to stick with it. If Monday is on your phone and Friday is in your day planner, it might feel like work.

- Once you have chosen your medium, all you have to do is write down what you want. Some people write in their journals to remember the natural things around them, others write down their deepest thoughts, and still, others just write down what happened during the day. Some people do all of those at the same time. If you want to write one minute about your dreams and the next about aliens, that's fine. Anything that will help you get your ideas on paper.

- Try to write in a journal every day. If you make it a habit, you'll keep doing it, and habits are formed when things are done every day. We keep a journal so we can make sense of the world around us and see things from a different point of view. It's not like you have to do homework every night. So put it in a time slot you have open every day or write a sentence here and there when you feel like it.

- Include cool facts and interesting things people say or do. You will have a record of some of the things you know for the rest of your life.

(University of Rochester Medical Center, 2019)

The Art of Travel Photography: Capturing Memories One Frame at a Time

One crucial aspect of travel that deserves its own spotlight is photography. Not just for those #TravelGram posts, but for preserving memories and telling stories of the places you've explored and the people you've met. If your phone's memory is anything like mine, it's brimming with travel photos. But are they all Instagram-worthy? Well, that's where this section comes in handy. Let's dive into some easy tips to elevate your travel photography game.

1. Know Your Equipment:

Whether you're using a DSLR, a point-and-shoot camera, or your smartphone, understanding the capabilities of your device is key. Explore different modes and settings before you embark on your trip. And remember, a great photo doesn't always depend on having the fanciest gear.

2. Light is Your Best Friend:

Good lighting can make or break a photo. The "golden hours"—just after sunrise or just before sunset—provide soft light that can result in spectacular shots. Midday light, on the other hand, can often be harsh and create strong shadows. Learning to use light to your advantage will vastly improve your photos.

3. Composition Matters:

Ever heard of the "rule of thirds"? Imagine a grid on your viewfinder and try to position the main subject of your photo at one of the intersections. This can create a more balanced and visually interesting shot. Also, consider different perspectives—shoot from high above, down at ground level, or even from the side.

4. Capture the Moment:

Photography is all about capturing moments. Don't just aim for landmarks, aim for emotions and actions too. A laughing local, a bustling market, or a quiet, cobblestoned alley can say as much about a place as its most famous monument.

5. Respect:

While capturing your surroundings, remember to respect the local people, their customs, and the environment. If you want to take a photo of a local, it's best to ask for permission first. Not only is it courteous, but it can also be a great way to engage and learn more about their culture.

6. Post-Processing:

A little editing can go a long way to enhance your photos. There are plenty of free editing tools and apps available that can help adjust exposure, contrast, saturation, and more. But remember, the aim is to enhance the photo, not completely transform it.

7. Practice, Practice, Practice:

Finally, the more photos you take, the better you'll become. Don't be disheartened if your photos don't come out as you hoped initially. The beauty of digital photography is that you can take countless photos to learn and improve.

Whether you're exploring a bustling city, trekking through the mountains, lounging by the sea, or discovering your own neighborhood, each photo you take is a record of your unique experience. As you traverse the globe, your photography skills will continue to grow, and your photos will be vibrant reminders of your adventures. So, start snapping, and let your photos tell the story of your journeys.

CHAPTER 10

FINDING YOUR TRIBE

H ow do people find their lifelong partners in crime? The truth is, they usually find you. People will always find others they consider friends, so whom you choose to be in your tribe depends on you.

A true friend is someone you can occasionally put more faith in than yourself to look out for your best interests. To find your tribe, you can simply go to places you like. Nature lovers go camping, visit botanical gardens, etc. If you want to find your people, they are probably where you want to go.

Simply being yourself and doing what you enjoy is all that is necessary. Traveling is also a good idea because it broadens your circle of friends and introduces you to people who may not share your background, religion, or style but who may share some of your core interests or values.

Cheers!

Wine and whisky, tequila and sangria—all these and every drink in between have one thing in common: They have the power to bring people together for a brilliant party. **I'm not advocating for you to start drinking on a regular basis, to drink more than is healthy, or to drink at all if you aren't of legal age where you live**, but any self-respecting connoisseur should be able to tell the difference between a good bottle of merlot and a good bottle of mezcal.

An interesting man knows how to properly entertain his friends without having to rely simply on shots and beer pong.

Here is your guide to everything drinks related, *hiccup*, enjoy:

Know your way around wine, especially when trying to impress your date in a restaurant.

Red wines:

- Cabernet sauvignon is a heavy-bodied wine made of dark, ripe fruit with hints of vanilla and spices. It goes really well with beef.

- Pinot noir is a light-bodied wine with hints of vanilla, a few spices, cherries, berries, and red fruits.

- Bordeaux red blends (Meritage), a heavy-bodied wine made of big, bold, strong, savory flavors.

- Malbec is a medium-bodied wine with hints of dark berry, cherry, cocoa, and black pepper spice flavors.

- Merlot is a medium-bodied wine with hints of raspberry and cherry.

White wines:

- Chardonnay, a medium-bodied white wine with a wide range of crisp, light flavors like lemon or tropical fruits.

- Sauvignon blanc is a medium- to medium-heavy-bodied wine with hints of green fruits, pears, etc. It goes great with seafood and chicken.

- Pinot Grigio/Pinot Gris–it's called Pinot Grigio in Italy and Pinot Gris in France but made from the same grapes. It has lime, pear, and sour apple flavors in Italy. It has lemon, honey, and honeysuckle flavors in France. In the U.S., the flavor palette has hints of ripe stone fruit and white nectarines.

- Rosé has a light to medium-heavy body with an array of different flavors depending on its body. Everything from summer fruits to floral spices.

(Backbar, n.d.)

Worldly Spirits

Triumphant tequila:

Tequila is a spirit made in Mexico from a specific type of agave called blue agave. Mezcal is a spirit made of any of the more than 50 types of agave, so tequila is a different type of mezcal.

While agave used to make tequila is typically steamed in ovens, agave used to make mezcal is frequently roasted in underground pits, which can give the spirit a distinct smoky note.

There are three types of tequila: Blanco, Reposado and Añejo

The most popular brands are: Jose Cuervo Tequila, Patrón Silver Tequila

Brilliant bourbons and whiskeys:

Whiskey is distilled grain mash. Different types of whiskey are bourbon, rye whiskey, scotch whisky, Canadian whisky, Japanese whisky, Tennessee whiskey, and Irish whiskey.

The most popular brands are Jack Daniels, Jameson, Maker's Mark, and Woodford Reserve.

Rambunctious rums:

A distilled liquor made of sugarcane, molasses or juice.

Types of rum include white rum, golden rum, dark rum, aged rum, coconut rum (more of a liqueur), spiced rum, and cachaça (a Brazilian rum).

The most popular brands are: Bacardi, Captain Morgan, Goslings Black Seal, Malibu Coconut, Tipo Tinto

Glorious gins:

A distilled liquor made of a type of grain or grapes. Predominantly, gin gets its flavor from juniper berries.

Types of gin include Tanqueray, London Dry, and Old Tom. These are also the popular brands.

Victorious vodkas:

Vodka is also a distilled liquor made of fermented grain, rye, wheat, potatoes, or sugar beet molasses.

Popular brands are: Tito's, Skyy, Absolut, and Smirnoff

Bombastic beer:

Beer is an alcohol made from fermenting cereal grains, most commonly barley. There are two types of beer ales and lagers. These two types are brewing methods.

The most common styles are:

Ales: Blonde ale, brown ale, pale ale, and India pale ale (IPA), sour ale, porter, and stout

Lager: American lager, lite lager, pilsner, wheat beer, amber, and dark lager

Every country has their different popular brands. The brands that have gained world renown are Stella Artois, Budweiser, Heineken, Guinness, and Corona.

For more on the different types of alcohol see the www.acouplecooks.com website (Overhiser, 2021).

Here are seven easy cocktails every man should know how to make when having a small get-together at home:

Negroni:

Ingredients: Campari, sweet vermouth, gin

Starter recipe:

1 oz London dry gin

1 oz sweet vermouth

1 oz Campari

Stir with ice for 20-30 seconds. Strain into coupe glass. Garnish with orange peel.

Gin and Tonic:

Ingredients: London Dry gin, tonic water, lime wedge

Starter recipe:

Gin (amount to preference)

Tonic water (amount to preference)

Pour over ice, garnish with lime wedge

Martini:

Ingredients: Gin or vodka, dry vermouth, orange bitters (optional for gin, not necessary for vodka)

Starter recipe:

2 oz gin

1 oz dry vermouth

Add contents to an ice-filled mixing glass or metal shaker. Stir, don't shake, for about 10 seconds. Strain into a coupe or cocktail glass and garnish with a lemon peel.

Manhattan:

Ingredients: Bourbon or rye whiskey, sweet vermouth, bitters

Starter recipe:

2 oz rye whiskey

1 oz sweet vermouth

2 dashes of Angostura bitters

Stir the ingredients with cracked ice, then strain into a chilled coupe. Garnish with an orange twist or brandied cherry (none of that cheap maraschino bullshit).

Daiquiri:

Ingredients: White rum, freshly squeezed lime juice, sugar

Starter recipe:

2 oz white rum

1 oz fresh-squeezed lime juice

¾ oz simple syrup

Combine ingredients in a mixing glass with ice and shake well. Strain into a coupe.

<u>**Margarita**</u>:

Ingredients: Blanco tequila, freshly squeezed lime juice, orange liqueur or triple sec

Starter recipe:

2 oz silver tequila

1 oz Cointreau

1 oz fresh-squeezed lime juice

Rub a lime wedge over the rim of a rocks glass (or Margarita glass) then twist on a plate of coarse salt so it attaches. Shake the ingredients with cracked ice, then strain them into a glass over ice.

<u>**Old Fashioned**</u>:

Ingredients:

1 teaspoon (5g) superfine sugar, toasted sugar, or 1 sugar cube

2 to 3 dashes of Angostura bitters

2 ounces (60ml) bourbon or rye whiskey

Orange and/or cocktail cherry

Combine whiskey, bitters, and sugar in a mixing glass. Add several large ice cubes and stir rapidly with a bar spoon to chill. Strain into a rocks glass with fresh ice. Garnish, if you like, with a slice of orange and/or a cherry.

Following the Code

There are boundaries that should never be crossed, and friend etiquette is a crucial component of any friendship. Understanding what is acceptable and unacceptable

behavior is crucial.

Friendship "don'ts" include:

- Avoid gossiping about friends. Instead, watch their back and never reveal the secrets they've confided in you. Here, the golden rule applies: If you don't want people to know about your private business, don't tell them about your friends'.

- Don't date their ex. This is a big deal-breaker in most if not all friendships. You should not lose a good friend because of a romantic interest who hasn't put in as much time and effort as your friend has over the years.

- Don't go on a date with your friend's crush if they ask you out. To avoid hurting their feelings, you should avoid dating the person your friend likes. This is an extremely painful and perplexing circumstance.

- Respect their privacy if they don't want to discuss something. When it's not the right time to push, you can usually tell. You are also aware of when a topic is best discussed. Keep this in mind, but when they say no, the best thing you can do is be there for them and show them they can open up when they feel the time is right.

- Don't belittle their choices. You are not their parents or their teachers. If they like something, you can express your opinion, but don't break down theirs. It is unhealthy for friendship, and it makes people clam up when they have an opinion or choice in the future.

- Do not agree or disagree with them when they complain about their spouse or partner. Rather, say nothing and nod or shrug. Relationships fluctuate; one day your friend can just be venting, and the next they can be angry at you for daring to say anything about their beloved. Steer clear of saying anything, as this might turn into a very sticky situation.

- Don't be deceitful or scheming. A friend is someone you can trust. If they don't trust you, how could you be their friend? Don't treat any relationship as a game.

- Don't make empty promises. A promise made to a friend helps to establish trust, which means you can rely on them to keep their end of the bargain.

- Don't monitor their behavior. They know when they have had enough. If they want to have it, it is their responsibility to know when they have enough, and your responsibility is to be there with and for them. You wouldn't want to be watched over all the time either.

- Don't judge them. If you disagree about something they did or think it was a bad idea, that is okay. But what is done is done. Telling them they were wrong will not solve their problem or change what has happened.

- If you or your friend feels that you have outgrown your friendship, end it. Don't let it linger. Your pain is mutual. Instead, cut things off completely and go about your lives. One day, if the friendship is worthwhile, things will turn out. Any relationship that is forced feels like work.

- Don't lie to your friend - ever. Not to protect them or yourself. If trust is betrayed, it's game over. Lies breed more lies.

Friendship dos include:

- Keep their secrets safe, they are theirs to tell. A relationship is strengthened and their trust is increased when secrets are shared.

- Respect their choices. We all have our histories and reasons for doing things. Their norms and values are just as important as yours. Respect that, and everything will be fine.

- Be honest but be tactful. If your friend confides in you about anything and becomes emotional while doing so, you should perhaps just listen and support them. Wait until later to speak before contributing what you have to say.

- Discuss potential problems as soon as they arise. Later fights will be horrible if you let things simmer. Tell them politely that you disagree with anything they do or say if you have a concern.

- Say what you mean and honor your commitments. It is more valuable than gold if they can believe what you say. If they require a straightforward answer to their issues, they will come to you.

- If you borrow it, give it back. Your friendship would benefit greatly if you returned their items after borrowing them and perhaps even gave them a small gift as a thank you. This could possibly prompt them to return the favor later.

- Give honest advice. Even if it hurts, honest advice is sometimes exactly what people need. Friends should be honest and help each other with both their deeds and words.

- Accept your limitations. It's acceptable if there is a situation you are unsure how to handle. We are not always expected to have all the solutions. As much as you can, assist others, then suggest that they seek out additional assistance from those who may have more knowledge or resources.

- Never take a true friend for granted or lose sight of their value. You can develop the self-assurance we all strive for with a true friend by your side. If you are fortunate enough to establish such a solid bond with someone, treasure it. From that point on, things can only get better. (Team, 2009)

CHAPTER 11

FINDING YOUR MATE FOR LIFE

F ALLING IN LOVE IS the best feeling in the world. The rush of endorphins and adoration of a new relationship or developing lasting love with someone is the most rewarding journey anyone can embark on. This chapter will hopefully help with this.

Here are some first-date suggestions to get you started:

- Visit an arcade, go go-karting, or engage in another enjoyable activity.

- Explore the outdoors by going fruit-picking, hiking, or going to a botanical garden.

- Visit an art gallery or a museum.

- Consider visiting an escape room or playing some friendly pool or attending a trivia night somewhere.

- Experience other modes of transportation, like a cable car, horseback riding, or paddle boats.

- Take a class together, like a cooking class or something else you enjoy.

- Do something artistic (e.g., ceramic, painting) (Ormont Blumberg, 2022).

Getting in Touch With Your Feelings

Emotional and Communication Skills Every Man Needs to Work On

- *Every man should know how to listen*
  Active listening is a skill. You can hear things but not properly take them in. It is very important in any relationship to know the difference.

- *Every man should know how to recognize his own feelings*
  The emotion wheel can be used in this instance again. Dealing with your feelings as soon as they come up, analyzing them, and working through them helps you express them to your partner.

- *Every man should know how to be vulnerable*
  The more time you spend with your partner the more emotions you have around them. If you can help them through their more vulnerable moments, allow them to see that side of you too. Be open and remember you can cry in front of them too. The tender moments are the important ones in a relationship.

- *Every man should be open to going to therapy*
  Go to therapy if you think you need more help or if you and your partner could benefit from it. The health of your mind is just as important as the health of your

body. Talk to your partner and find out who can help. You should be willing to go if your partner wants to. Keep in mind that they want to work on the relationship, which shows they care.

- *Every man should know how to apologize*
  In every relationship, there are moments when you might make a mistake. Knowing when and how to apologize makes the relationship stronger. Don't let things brew, open, kind communication makes you man enough to own up to your mistakes.

- *Every man should know how to grow*
  Every step you take towards an open, honest relationship makes you grow as a person. Allow for that growth during and after good or bad instances. Learn from what you can, allow it in, and if needed let it out.

- *Every man should know how to help his partner achieve an orgasm*
  Don't be afraid to ask questions or let your partner guide you through their needs. Doing your research can be beneficial too. I don't mean pornographic materials; they are surprisingly deceiving. Reading articles on pleasuring your partner is a better way to go.

$$\bullet \; \bullet \; \bullet \; \bullet \; \bullet \; \bullet \; \bullet \; \bullet \; \bullet \; \bullet$$

Just Getting in Touch

Online dating dos and don'ts

How to stay safe:

- Be yourself, but protect yourself. Don't pretend to be someone you're not; no catfishing, but don't give too much personal information out too freely.

- Remember who you are. It is easy to get discouraged if you like someone and they "ghost" you or you swipe right and they swipe left. Don't take it personally, everyone has someone out there for them. Just focus on yourself. If you are ready to date then you should have a strong level of self-love. Remember: if you love yourself 100% then you need someone who will love you 110%, and we all deserve a love like that.

- Don't be afraid to stop everything if there are one or two red flags. You may have things to deal with from past relationships. Don't quickly dismiss what you've learned in the past. Your past pain might make you see the new relationship in a bad light. If that happens, there might be a reason for it, and it's important to make sure that doesn't happen again.

- Remember it is a marathon not a sprint. Start off slow, be charming, work up to the bigger things and just get to know them. At the beginning everything happens fast but building a relationship means that you lay brick after brick. Don't rush it; enjoy the journey.

- Don't start off sending "THAT" picture. There, I said it! You know which picture I'm talking about. No one on this Earth wants to meet the one-eyed monster right at the start of a conversation. If you don't know the person, don't show them the goods, and if the urge gets too strong, for the love of Pete, don't put your face in the picture. Help them use their imagination, and don't give it away. It builds up the tension and gives you something to think about before you find out what's going on in the bedroom. (Perez, 2021)

What to ask before meeting in real life:

1. What are you looking for?

2. Do you have any siblings?

3. Are you from around here?

4. What do you like to do for fun?

5. Do you drink? What's your favorite drink?

6. What are you watching on Netflix, if you have an account?

7. What's your most embarrassing moment?

8. Do you like to read? What are you reading?

9. What do you do for a living?

10. Would you rather... or...?

11. How would you react in a zombie apocalypse?

12. What music do you like? Who is your favorite artist?

13. What's your favorite outdoor activity?

14. Who are you closest with in your family?

15. Do you have any pets? (Jawed, 2017)

• • • ● ● • ● ● • • •

Learn more about how different attachment styles interact when it comes to love, relationships and dating.

Click on this link or scan the QR code below.

Attachment Styles 101:
Love, Relationship &
Dating Course

Conclusion

With that, we have unfortunately come to the end of your guided tour through adulting. This guide hopefully helped as much as intended and the support is appreciated.

In Closing

In these strange times, it can be really hard to be a man. Everyone has challenges in life, but fortunately, there is always someone there to help. Remember that you're at a stage in your life where you should enjoy the little things and make your own mistakes so you can learn from them. These tools are here for you, but if you forget one or two and still find a way to take charge of a situation on your own, you are well on your way to adulting hard. Use the workbook and bonus materials that are offered along with the book, and put yourself first. Enjoy living your life. Check the references if you need more information, and give this book to someone who needs it. This book is part of the *Adulting Hard* series, so keep an eye out for them and feel free to pick up the next one as you go. Have a great life!

Thank you!

Jeffrey

Leave a Review

If you loved this or any other of my books, please leave a positive review by visiting https://www.amazon.com/review/create-review/?ie=UTF8&channel=glance-detail&asin=B0BW8H8CLC. It would mean the world to me

CHAPTER 12

GLOSSARY OF COOKING TERMS:

AL DENTE: PASTA THAT you cook slightly, it is still firm but soft enough to eat.

Bake: To cook food with dry heat in the oven. Not meat mainly dishes involving dough or batter.

Barbecue: To cook food over a fire or hot coals.

Baste: To wet food while cooking for moisture and flavor.

Batter: An uncooked runny mixture that makes a dish after getting firm while baking.

Beat: To rapidly stir a mixture until it gets smooth, using a whisk, spoon, or mixer.

Blend: To combine 2 or more ingredients well.

Boil: To cook food in bubbling water at the water's boiling point. (212 degrees Fahrenheit or 100 degrees Celsius).

Bone: To take out the bones from any meat.

Braise: To first brown meat, then cook over low heat in a small amount of liquid in a covered pan until soft.

Bread: To roll food in an egg mixture and then crumbs or cornmeal before cooking.

Broil: To cook meat or fish over high heat in an oven.

Brown: To cook food on top of the stove until browned.

Caramelize: To melt sugar in a pan until it is golden or brown syrup.

Core: To remove the centers from fruits and vegetables with a knife or corer.

Cream: To mix ingredients like sugar and butter together until light and fluffy.

Cube: To cut food into small cubes.

Cut in: To add butter to flour by cutting the butter into tiny pieces with 2 knives, kitchen shears or a pastry blender.

Deep-fry: To cook by heating large amounts of a fat or cooking oil and adding the food.

Dice: To cut food into tiny cubes. Much smaller than to cube.

Dress: To add dressing to a salad or to ready meat for cooking.

Drizzle: To pour liquid in spirals over food in a fine stream.

Dust: To coat lightly with different powdery ingredients.

Fillet: To cut the bones from a piece of meat.

Flambé: To drizzle liquor over food and ignite it before serving.

Fold: To combine light, wet ingredients with a heavier, dry mixture, using a gentle over-and-under motion.

Glaze: To coat foods with jellies, sauces, or syrups for a shiny finish and extra flavor.

Grate: To rub foods against a grater to get shredded bits.

Grease: To rub the inside of a cooking dish or pan with fat to stop food from sticking to it.

Grill: To cook food on a rack over direct heat like fire or coals.

Grind: To break down food into a powder using a grinder or a food processor.

Knead: To blend dough with your hands to make it more pliable.

Marinate: To soak the meat in a flavored liquid, readying it for a more flavor-filled roast or grill.

Mince: To break down meat or other foods into tiny bits with a knife or meat grinder.

Parboil: To partially cook by boiling and then using another method for finishing or crisping food.

Poach: To cook over very low heat in barely simmering water.

Purée: To break down food until it is in liquid or near liquid form.

Reduce: To thicken and then boil a liquid.

Roast: To cook food with dry heat in an oven.

Sauté or pan fry: To cook food in a little bit of fat over high heat.

Sear: To brown the surface of meat by quick-cooking over high heat to seal in the meat's juices.

Shred: To cut food into narrow strips with a knife or a grater.

Simmer: To cook in liquid just below the boiling point. Small bubbles form but don't bubble up.

Steam: To cook food on a rack using water vapor.

Stew: To cook over low heat in a liquid, closed in a pot.

Whisk: To beat ingredients with a fork or whisk until mixed and fluffy.

(Dictionary of Cooking Terms, 2007)

CHAPTER 13

REFERENCES

10 Travel Hacks You Must Know About. (2022, May 25). Travel Blog: Travel Tips, Tricks & More by Cleartrip. https://www.cleartrip.com/collections/best-travel-hacks/

30 Books Every Man Should Read By 30. (2020, March 13). Esquire. https://www.esquire.com/uk/culture/books/g4898/30-books-every-man-should-read-by-30/

30+ Stylish TV Shows Every Man Should Binge. (2022, December 1). Realmenrealstyle.com. https://www.realmenrealstyle.com/most-stylish-tv-shows-men-watch/

Abraham, L. (2019, June 28). *These Crispy Air Fryer Sweet Potato Fries Are Completely Irresistible.* Delish. https://www.delish.com/cooking/recipe-ideas/a28136123/air-fryer-sweet-potato-recipe/

American Psychological Association. (2017, July). What Is Cognitive Behavioral Therapy? *American Psychological Association.* https://www.apa.org/ptsd-guideline/patients-and-families/cognitive-behavioral

Anonymous. (2022, August 24). *I'm living in a house-share at 65 – there are a lot of people in the UK like me | Anonymous.* The Guardian.

https://www.theguardian.com/commentisfree/2022/aug/24/living-in-a-houseshare-council-flat

Austin, J. (2021, May 13). How to Clean a Toilet the Right Way. *The New York Times.* https://www.nytimes.com/wirecutter/guides/how-to-clean-toilet/

Backbar. (n.d.). *Basic Wine Knowledge Guide.* Www.getbackbar.com. https://www.getbackbar.com/basic-wine-knowledge

Best before, use by and sell by dates explained. (2021, September 12). Www.eufic.org. https://www.eufic.org/en/food-safety/article/best-before-use-by-and-sell-by-dates-explained

Buswell, G. (2014). *Healthcare in the UK: a guide to the NHS and the UK healthcare system | Expatica.* Expat Guide to the United Kingdom | Expatica; Expat Guide to the United Kingdom | Expatica. https://www.expatica.com/uk/healthcare/healthcare-basics/the-national-health-service-and-health-insurance-in-the-uk-1092057/

Caldwell, M. (2021, November 15). *7 Questions to Ask Before You Make That Big Purchase.* The Balance. https://www.thebalancemoney.com/before-you-make-large-purchases-2385817

Cammarata, J., & Eating well. (2022, February 10). *8 Foods You Should Never Freeze.* EatingWell. https://www.eatingwell.com/article/7740165/foods-you-should-never-freeze/

Common Scams | Office of the Attorney General. (n.d.). Www.texasattorneygeneral.gov. https://www.texasattorneygeneral.gov/consumer-protection/common-scams

Console Jr., R. P. (2021, March 25). *10 Tips to Avoid Accidents in Your Home.* The National Law Review. https://www.natlawreview.com/article/10-tips-to-avoid-accidents-your-home

Cooks-Campbell, A. (2022, April 20). *The Emotion Wheel: How to Use it to Get to Know Yourself.* Www.betterup.com. https://www.betterup.com/blog/emotion-wheel

Cooper, R. (n.d.). *25 movies every man should see*

before he's 25. JOE.ie. Retrieved December 21, 2022, from
https://www.joe.ie/movies-tv/25-movies-every-man-see-hes-25-555999

Cussen, M. P. (2022, January 21). *The Best Investments for Young Adults.* Investopedia.
https://www.investopedia.com/articles/younginvestors/12/best-investments-for-young
-people.asp

Dictionary of Cooking Terms. (2007, April 12). Good Housekeeping; Good
Housekeeping.
https://www.goodhousekeeping.com/food-recipes/cooking/tips/a16958/dictionary-co
oking-terms/

Doherty, R. (2021, June 26). *How to paint a wall: 15
steps to painting a wall like a pro.* Homesandgardens.com.
https://www.homesandgardens.com/advice/how-to-paint-a-wall

Draghici, A. (2018, August 1). *Top 10 Questions to Ask a Potential Roommate.* RentCafe
Rental Blog.
https://www.rentcafe.com/blog/apartmentliving/tips-tricks-renters/top-10-questions-a
sk-potential-roommate

Hamby, B., & Mueller, J. (2022, June 24). *Negotiate with the
Finance Manager at a Car Dealership and Save Money.* WikiHow.
https://www.wikihow.com/Deal-with-the-Finance-Manager-at-Car-Dealership

Health. (2019, February). *About private health insurance.* Australian Government
Department of Health and Aged Care.
https://www.health.gov.au/topics/private-health-insurance/about-private-health-insura
nce

Health insurance 101: How does health insurance work in Canada? (n.d.). Canada Life.
https://www.canadalife.com/insurance/health-and-dental-insurance/how-does-health-i
nsurance-work.html

Hold Mail - Stop Mail Delivery Online | USPS. (n.d.). Www.usps.com. Retrieved
December 6, 2022, from https://www.usps.com/manage/hold-mail.htm

How to Iron Clothes - Step by Step. (2019, December 17). Cleanipedia PH.

https://www.cleanipedia.com/ph/clothing-care/learn-how-to-iron-clothes-the-easy-way
.html

How To Prevent Fire In Your Home. (2018, January 9). StaySafe.org.
https://staysafe.org/how-to-prevent-fire-in-your-home/

How to Prevent the Most Common Household Accident. (n.d.).
GoHealth Urgent Care. Retrieved December 20, 2022, from
https://www.gohealthuc.com/library/how-prevent-most-common-household-accident

How U.S. Health Insurance Works | Vaden Health Services. (n.d.). Vaden.stanford.edu.
https://vaden.stanford.edu/insurance-referral-office/health-insurance-overview/how-us
-health-insurance-works

Hoyt, A. (2010, September 9). *10 Quick Tips for Removing Stains from Clothing.*
HowStuffWorks.
https://home.howstuffworks.com/home-improvement/household-hints-tips/cleaning-
organizing/10-quick-tips-for-removing-stains-from-clothing.htm

Investopedia. (2022, June 22). *Who Needs Renters Insurance?* Investopedia.
https://www.investopedia.com/insurance/renters-insurance/

Jackery team. (2022, March 30). *How To Survive a Natural Disaster (The Survival Kit
Guide).* Jackery.
https://www.jackery.com/blogs/news/how-to-survive-a-natural-disaster-the-survival-kit
-guide

Jawed, E. (2017, October 20). *17 Essential Questions You Must Ask Your Online Match
Before Meeting Them IRL - Narcity.* Www.narcity.com.
https://www.narcity.com/17-essential-questions-you-must-ask-your-online-match-befo
re-meeting-them-irl

Knox Finley, J. (2020, September 17). *30 Questions to
Ask a Roommate Before You Move in Together.* MyDomaine.
https://www.mydomaine.com/questions-to-ask-a-potential-roommate

Kylstra, C. (2014, October 21). *20 Healthy Habits You Should Adopt In Your Twenties.*
BuzzFeed; BuzzFeed. https://www.buzzfeed.com/carolynkylstra/healthy-living-habits

Leshnower, R. (2022, February 18). *The Pros and Cons of Living With Roommates*. The Spruce.
https://www.thespruce.com/should-i-live-with-roommates-or-live-alone-156440#:~:tex
t=There%20are%20many%20good%20reasons

Masterclass. (2021, July 7). *5 Different Types of Wall Paint and Finishes*. Masterclass.
https://www.masterclass.com/articles/different-types-of-wall-paint-and-finishes

Menon, L. (2021, August 9). *50 Travel Hacks That Will Change The Way You Travel Forever*. Headout Blog. https://www.headout.com/blog/ultimate-travel-hacks/

Milliken, M. (2022, August 26). *12 Easy Ways to Cut Expenses at Home*. Debt.org.
https://www.debt.org/advice/how-to-cut-expenses/

Miyashiro, L. (2018, December 7). *FINALLY A Protein Ball That Doesn't Taste Extremely Artificial*. Delish.
https://www.delish.com/cooking/recipe-ideas/a25416301/protein-balls-recipe/

Nast, C. (2022, September 13). *This Is the Best Skin Care Routine for Men (Even for Beginners)*. GQ. https://www.gq.com/story/best-skin-care-routine-for-men

NHS. (2021, February 2). *Breathing exercises for stress*. Nhs.uk.
https://www.nhs.uk/mental-health/self-help/guides-tools-and-activities/breathing-exer
cises-for-stress/

Ormont Blumberg, P. (2022, August 26). *The 20 best first date ideas, according to relationship experts*. TODAY.com.
https://www.today.com/life/relationships/first-date-ideas-rcna44970

Overhiser, S. (2021, May 30). *Types of Alcohol & Liquor Names*. A Couple Cooks.
https://www.acouplecooks.com/types-of-alcohol-liquor-names/

Perez, J. M.-A. (2021, January 30). *The dos and don'ts of online dating apps*. The Bakersfield Californian.
https://www.bakersfield.com/bakersfield-life/the-dos-and-donts-of-online-dating-apps/
article_34a0cfe6-4182-11eb-807f-bf3c8ebef280.html

Ramsey Insurance. (2022, August 15). How Much Car Insurance Do I Need? Ramsey

Solutions. https://www.ramseysolutions.com/insurance/how-much-car-insurance

Reyes, M., & Matthews, M. (2016, January 4). *10 Incredible Health Benefits to Masturbation*. Men's Health; Men's Health. https://www.menshealth.com/sex-women/a19534050/5-reasons-you-should-masturba te-tonight/

SeiderTeam. (2018, July 20). *6 Steps Any Homeowner Can Take to Fix a Clogged Drain*. Seider Heating - Plumbing - Electrical. https://www.seider.com/6-steps-to-unclog-a-backed-up-drain/#:~:text=Try%20boiling %20water%20and%20salt

SouthFloridaReporter.com. (2017, November 17). *Americans Consume An Average 53 Pounds Of Bread A Year*. South Florida Reporter. https://southfloridareporter.com/americans-consume-average-53-pounds-bread-year/

Stanley, M. (2020, November 5). *How to Fill Holes in Wall*. MYMOVE. https://www.mymove.com/home-inspiration/diy/how-to-fill-holes-in-wall/

Stelter, G. (2016, October 4). *Chakras: A Beginner's Guide to the 7 Chakras*. Healthline. https://www.healthline.com/health/fitness-exercise/7-chakras#Chakra-101

Team, C. (2009, April 2). *Friendship dos and don'ts*. Cosmopolitan. https://www.cosmopolitan.com/uk/more/a5614/friendship-dos-donts-89915/

U.S. News. (2019). *The 30 World's Best Places to Visit*. Usnews.com. https://travel.usnews.com/rankings/worlds-best-vacations/

University of Rochester Medical Center. (2019). *Journaling for Mental Health*. Rochester.edu. https://www.urmc.rochester.edu/encyclopedia/content.aspx?ContentID=4552&Cont entTypeID=1

Watson, S. (2015, July 13). *First Aid Tips*. WebMD; WebMD. https://www.webmd.com/first-aid/first-aid-tips

What is a share house? (n.d.). Oakhouse. Retrieved December 5, 2022, from https://www.oakhouse.jp/eng/sharehouse#letsgomodal

Winston, A. (2016, July 8). *Six of the best co-living developments from around the world.* Dezeen; Dezeen.
https://www.dezeen.com/2016/07/08/six-best-co-living-developments-around-the-world/

ALSO BY JEFFREY C. CHAPMAN

Hello there! As an author, I know just how important reviews are for getting the word out about my work. When readers leave a review on Amazon, it helps others discover my book and decide whether it's right for them. Plus, it gives me valuable feedback on what readers enjoyed and what they didn't. So if you've read my book and enjoyed it (or even if you didn't!), I would really appreciate it if you took a moment to leave a review on Amazon. It doesn't have to be long or complicated - just a few words about what you thought of the book would be incredibly helpful. Thank you so much for your support!

Adulting Hard for Young Women

Adulting Hard After College

Adulting Hard in Your Late Twenties and Thirties

Made in the USA
Columbia, SC
19 July 2024

38992512R00104